The Most Important Story

BIBLE

The Most Important Story

BIBLE

Triumphs, Tragedies, Heroes, Miracles, and much more!

This illustrated children's Bible takes you on an exciting journey through the Bible. At the end of the book, "The Most Important Story Ever Told" will tell you what all this means to you personally and how you can begin the greatest adventure of your life!

WORLDSERVE
MINISTRIES

Published by WorldServe Ministries—www.worldserve.org

USA	Canada
PO Box 700787	PO Box 71505
Dallas, TX 75370	White Rock, BC V4B 5J5

Printed in Singapore, 2002

A Word to Parents

For the best start in life, your child needs a foundation of God's truth. It will provide a framework for making right choices and living life the way God intended. As the apostle Paul wrote to his young co-worker Timothy, "You have been taught the holy Scriptures from childhood, and they have given you the wisdom to receive the salvation that comes by trusting in Christ Jesus" (2 Timothy 3:15).

This illustrated Bible provides an exciting way to help children know the all-powerful God who performed mighty miracles on behalf of his people. He parted the Red Sea, stopped the floodwaters of the Jordan River and brought down the walls of Jericho.

Children will also come to know God as a loving heavenly Father who tenderly cares for ordinary people. Baby Moses was rescued from the Nile River, and a large crowd of people ate their fill when Jesus blessed five loaves of bread and two fish—the picnic of one small boy. God spoke to the boy Samuel in an audible voice, and God gave an amazing victory to David, a youngster who dared to fight for the honor of God's name. Esther was an orphan girl who became queen, a position she used to save her people from destruction. God had plans for each of these children before they were born, just as he has good plans for every child today.

This book is designed to help parents teach even small children to know God for themselves, and to have the assurance that they can trust him at every stage of their lives.

Our prayer is that God will bless and inspire you and your children as you read this special book.

Table of Contents

The New Testament

Creation

(Genesis 1–2)

In the beginning, God created the heavens and the earth. The earth didn't have any shape. It was empty and dark.

God spoke and whatever he said came into being. He said, "Let there be light," and there was light. He made the sky, the land, and the seas. And he made every kind of plant. Then God made the sun, moon, and stars to shine down on the earth.

The LORD God planted a garden in the east, in Eden. He made all kinds of trees grow out of the ground. Their fruit was good to eat. In the middle of the garden was the tree that gives life forever. The tree that gives the ability to tell the difference between good and evil was also there. At that time, the LORD God hadn't sent any rain, so a river flowed from the earth and watered the garden.

Then God made creatures to live in this wonderful place. He formed all the wild animals and the birds of the air out of the earth. He made all kinds of creatures that move along the ground. He made all the fish and every other living thing.

God saw everything he had made. And it was very good.

Adam and Eve in the Garden

(Genesis 1–2)

After God had made everything, he said, "Let's make people to be like ourselves." So God formed a man out of the dust of the ground. He breathed the breath of life into him, and the man became a living person. He was called Adam, which means "the man."

God put Adam in the Garden of Eden. He gave him this warning, "You can eat the fruit of any tree in the garden. But you mustn't eat the fruit of the tree that gives you the ability to tell between good and evil. If you do, you'll die."

Then God said, "It's not good for the man to be alone. I'll make a companion who will help him." So God caused Adam to sleep. While he was sleeping, God took out one of his ribs and closed up the opening. Then the LORD God made a woman from the rib and brought her to Adam. He was delighted and called her "Eve."

So God created people to be like him.

God blessed them. He said, "Have children and increase in number. Fill the earth and bring it under your control."

Adam and Eve looked after the garden. They were happy and enjoyed God's love as his children. Then one day...

Adam and Eve Sin

(Genesis 3)

Satan came to the garden disguised as a snake. He'd been an important angel but he became proud. He wanted to be above God. So he was thrown out of heaven. Now he wanted Adam and Eve to listen to him instead of to God.

He said to Eve, "Did God really say, 'You mustn't eat the fruit from any tree in the garden'?"

Eve replied, "God did say, 'You must not eat the fruit from the tree in the middle of the garden. If you do, you'll die.'"

"You won't die," he said. "You'll be like God."

Eve saw that the fruit was good to eat, and it would make a person wise. So she took some of the fruit and ate it. She also gave some to her husband, who was with her. And he ate it.

Suddenly, they were afraid. They hid from God. They'd done what he told them not to do. That's sin. With sin, death came into the world.

God sent Adam and Eve out of the Garden of Eden and away from him.

Because they were the very first people, all of us since then have been born sinful, outside of God's presence. How terrible! But even back then God had a plan. He promised that a man, one of Eve's descendants, would crush the snake's head.

Cain and Abel

(Genesis 4)

Adam and Eve had two sons, Cain and Abel. At harvest time, Cain brought his farm produce as an offering to the LORD. But Abel brought some of the best lambs from his flock.

The LORD was pleased with Abel and his offering. But he wasn't pleased with Cain and his offering. So Cain became very angry.

God loved Cain. He spoke to him. "Why are you angry? Do what's right. Then I'll welcome you." But Cain wouldn't listen. He attacked his brother Abel and killed him.

The LORD said to Cain, "Where's your brother Abel?"

"I don't know," he replied. "Am I supposed to keep track of my brother?"

But God knew what Cain had done and punished him for his sin.

This murder was just the beginning of the evil things people would do because they were separated from God. More and more people were born, and hardly anyone wanted to obey God. But many years later, one man pleased God fully and did exactly what he wanted.

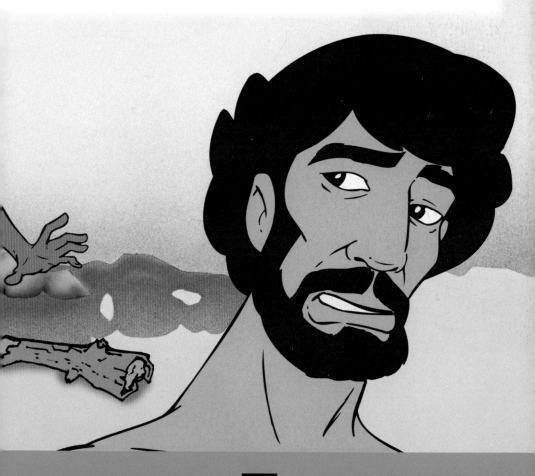

Noah and the Ark

(Genesis 6–7, 9)

The LORD saw how bad people had become, doing all kinds of evil things. He was very sad that he'd made human beings, and his heart was filled with pain.

But the LORD was pleased with Noah. Noah loved him and did what was right. So God said to Noah, "Make yourself an ark, a big wooden boat. I'm going to bring a flood on the earth. Everything on earth will die. Go into the ark with your family. Take with you two of every living thing, male and female, with food for all of you. They'll be kept alive with you."

Noah did everything exactly as God commanded him.

When the birds and animals were in the ark, it rained. For 40 days and 40 nights the flood kept coming. All the animals and creatures and every human being died. Only Noah and those with him in the ark were saved.

When the waters went down, God made a promise to Noah. He said, "I now make a covenant, a special agreement, with you and with everyone who'll be born after you: Never again will a flood destroy all life on the earth. I've put my rainbow in the clouds. It will be the sign of this covenant. Whenever I see the rainbow, I'll remember."

Abraham and Sarah

(Genesis 12, 15, 17)

Noah's family grew until there were lots of people in the world again. God chose a man named Abram for the next part of his plan.

He told him, "Leave your country and your people. Go to the land I'll show you. All nations on earth will be blessed because of you."

Abram did as God said and set out with his wife. But he had no children and he was an old man.

Then the LORD took Abram outside and said, "Look up at the sky. Count the stars, if you can. That's how many children you'll have." Abram believed the LORD, and the LORD was pleased with him and declared him righteous because of his faith.

The LORD made a covenant, a special agreement, with Abram. He promised, "I'm giving this land to you and your children and children's children forever."

God also chose Sarai, Abram's wife. He said, I'll bless Sarai and she will have a son. She'll be the mother of nations. Kings of nations will come from her." God changed their names to Abraham and Sarah.

When Abraham was 100 years old and Sarah was 90, the baby God had promised was born. They called him Isaac.

Isaac
(Genesis 22)

Some years later God tested Abraham's faith and obedience. God said, "Take your son, Isaac, whom you love so much. Give him to me as a burnt offering. Sacrifice him on one of the mountains I will point out to you."

Abraham put the wood for the burnt offering on his son, Isaac. He himself carried the fire and the knife. "We'll be back," he told his servants.

Isaac didn't understand what was happening. "Where's the lamb for the burnt offering?" he asked.

Abraham answered, "God will provide a lamb, my son."

When they reached the place, Abraham built an altar and got ready to sacrifice Isaac. But the angel of the LORD shouted to him from heaven. "Stop, Abraham! Now I know you that you truly respect God. You didn't refuse to give me the son you love." Abraham looked up. He saw a ram caught in a bush nearby and sacrificed it instead.

The angel called again to Abraham from heaven, "This is what the LORD says: I vow by my own self that I will bless you richly. Through your children and children's children, all nations on earth will be blessed—all because you have done as I told you."

Jacob and Esau

(Genesis 25, 27)

When Isaac grew up, he married Rebekah. He prayed for her because she couldn't have children. The LORD answered his prayer, and she had twins, Esau first and then Jacob.

In those days, fathers used to pray a blessing for their eldest son. But Rebekah wanted Jacob to get the blessing. When Isaac was old and blind, Rebekah helped Jacob steal the blessing from Esau.

One day, when Esau was out hunting, she prepared some tasty food just the way Isaac liked it. She took Esau's best clothes and put them on Jacob. She covered his hands and neck with goatskins. (Esau was a hairy man.) Then she sent Jacob to Isaac with the tasty food and the bread she had made.

So Jacob pretended to be Esau. Isaac touched him and said, "This voice is Jacob's. But these hands are Esau's." Isaac didn't recognize him, so he gave Jacob his blessing.

Then Esau came back, bringing food for his father. When he realized what had happened, Esau let out a bitter cry. He begged Isaac to bless him, too. But it was too late.

Jacob's Family

(Genesis 27–31, 33, 35, 37)

Esau was very angry with Jacob. So Jacob ran away to his uncle. There he worked as a shepherd and married Leah and Rachel. They were Abraham's relatives, too. Jacob had twelve sons—Reuben, Simeon, Levi, Judah, Dan, Naphtali, Gad, Asher, Issachar, Zebulun, Joseph, and Benjamin—and a daughter, Dinah.

After 20 years the LORD told Jacob to return home. He set off with his family and servants on the long journey back. God came to Jacob when he was alone. He changed Jacob's name to Israel and blessed him. One day soon after this, Jacob looked up and saw Esau coming with 400 men! Jacob was very afraid. But Esau ran to meet Jacob. He threw his arms around him and kissed him.

Finally, Jacob came home to his father, Isaac. Isaac lived to be 180 years old.

Jacob stayed in the land that God had promised to give his family. At that time it was called the land of Canaan. And Jacob loved Joseph more than any of his other sons because Joseph had been born when he was old.

Joseph, the Dreamer

(Genesis 37, 39)

When Joseph was 17, his father gave him a multicolored robe. But Joseph's brothers hated him because they saw that Jacob loved him the most.

Joseph said to his brothers, "Listen to the dream I had. We were tying up bundles of grain. Suddenly my bundle stood up. Your bundles bowed down to it."

They understood the dream and said, "Will you really rule over us?" So they hated him even more.

One day Jacob sent Joseph to the fields to see his brothers.

They saw him coming and decided to get rid of him. They tore his beautiful robe and sold him to some traders going to Egypt. Then they told their father that Joseph was dead. Jacob was heartbroken.

The men sold Joseph to Potiphar, an important man in Egypt. The LORD gave Joseph success in everything he did. So Potiphar put Joseph in charge of his house.

After a while, Potiphar's wife noticed Joseph. She wanted him to fall in love with her. But he said, "No! My master trusts me. You're his wife. So how could I do an evil thing like that? How could I sin against God?" One day she lied to Potiphar about Joseph, and Potiphar became very angry. He put Joseph in prison.

Joseph, the Egyptian Ruler

(Genesis 41–42, 45–46, 50)

Pharaoh was Egypt's king. He dreamed that seven skinny cows ate seven fat cows. He heard Joseph understood dreams. So Joseph was brought from prison. God told Joseph the dream meant there would be seven years with lots of food in the land, then seven without—a terrible famine.

Joseph gave Pharaoh a plan to make sure there was enough food. Pharaoh liked it so much he put Joseph in charge of it. Joseph became the second most important man in Egypt.

The years passed, the famine came, and Jacob's family in Canaan needed food. Joseph's brothers went to Egypt to buy grain. When they arrived, they bowed down to Joseph. Joseph recognized them, but they didn't recognize him. Then Joseph remembered his dream.

At first he pretended not to know them. But the second time they came, he burst out, "I'm your brother Joseph, the one you sold into Egypt. Don't be angry with yourselves. You planned to harm me. But God planned it for good. He wanted to save many lives."

When Jacob heard Joseph was alive he was thrilled. God spoke to him, "Don't be afraid to go to Egypt. There I'll make you into a great nation. I'll go with you. I'll bring your people back again."

So Joseph met Jacob again. And he threw his arms around his father and cried for a long time.

Moses, the Child

(Exodus 1–2)

Jacob's family grew into a nation in Egypt. The Egyptians called them Hebrews. They were well-treated because of Joseph. But long after Joseph died, a new Pharaoh made them slaves. He ordered all baby Hebrew boys to be killed. He was afraid the Hebrews would become strong and rebel.

A Hebrew woman in the family of Levi gave birth to a son. She saw that he was a fine child, so she hid him. When she couldn't hide him any longer, she got a basket and placed the child in it. She put the basket in the Nile River.

Soon after this, Pharaoh's daughter went to the Nile to take a bath. She saw the basket. When she opened it, she saw the baby. He was crying, and she felt sorry for him. His sister, who was watching, came up to her and asked, "Should I go and find a Hebrew woman to nurse the baby for you?" Then she called the baby's real mother! The princess let her look after him until he was older. After that, the princess adopted him as her son. She named him Moses.

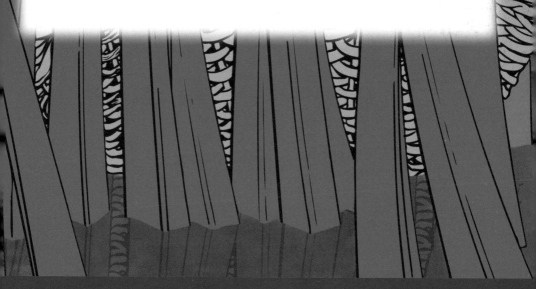

Moses and the Burning Bush

(Exodus 2–4)

When Moses had grown up, he saw an Egyptian hitting a Hebrew man. He didn't see anyone else. So he killed the Egyptian and hid his body in the sand.

Pharaoh heard what had happened and tried to kill Moses. But Moses escaped to a land far away.

Forty years later, Moses saw a strange sight in the desert. A bush was on fire, but it wasn't burning up! God spoke to Moses from inside the bush. "Take off your sandals. You're standing on holy

ground. I am the God of Abraham, Isaac, and Jacob." When Moses heard that, he was afraid.

The LORD said, "I've seen my people, the Israelites, suffering in Egypt. So I've come to save them from the Egyptians. I'll lead them out of that land into a rich, good land. I'm sending you to Pharaoh to bring them out of Egypt."

God promised to go with Moses. He told him what to say. He gave Moses miracles he could do to prove he was telling the truth. When Moses threw down his wooden staff, it changed into a snake! When he grabbed hold of the snake's tail, it turned back into a staff.

God also sent Moses' brother, Aaron, to help Moses.

The Plagues

(Exodus 4, 7–10)

Back in Egypt, Moses and Aaron gathered together all the leaders of Israel. Aaron told them everything the LORD had said. He did the miracles. Then the leaders believed that the LORD cared about them, and they worshiped him.

The LORD told Moses, "Pharaoh will refuse to listen to you, so I'll do many miracles in Egypt. Then the Egyptians will know that I am the LORD."

Moses asked Pharaoh to let the Israelites come out of Egypt. But Pharaoh refused. Because of this, God sent ten terrible plagues. Moses stretched out his wooden staff, and God turned all Egypt's water into blood. Next, frogs came out of the streams and covered the land. Then the dust of Egypt became biting gnats.

Pharaoh's magicians said, "God has done this." But Pharaoh wouldn't listen.

God filled the country with flies, a fourth plague. After that, all the Egyptian livestock died. Then boils broke out on people and animals. Next came the hail. It was the worst storm in Egypt's history.

Then God sent huge grasshoppers to eat what was left in the fields.

But the LORD made Pharaoh's heart hard. He wouldn't let the people of Israel go. So total darkness covered Egypt for three days. But there was light as usual where the people of Israel lived.

The Passover and Exodus

(Exodus 11–12)

The LORD said, "I'll send one more plague. After that, Pharaoh will let you go. About midnight I'll go through Egypt. Every eldest Egyptian son will die. I'll judge all their false gods. I am the LORD."

Moses sent for the leaders of Israel. He said, "Each family must kill a Passover lamb. Put some of its blood on the top and both sides of the door frame of the house. No one is allowed to go out until morning. The LORD will go through the land to strike

the Egyptians. He'll see the blood on the door frames and pass over. He won't let the destroying angel kill you."

Moses told the people never to forget what God would do. The people worshiped God and did as Moses said.

At midnight the Lord struck dead every eldest son in Egypt.

Then finally Pharaoh sent for Moses and Aaron. He said, "Get out of here, you and the Israelites! Go!"

The Lord's people had lived in Egypt for 430 years. Now they marched out of Egypt like an army. There were over 600,000 men, plus women and children!

Crossing the Red Sea

(Exodus 14)

After the Israelites left, Pharaoh had second thoughts. Pharaoh and his top men said, "What have we done? We've lost our slaves and the work they used to do for us!"

The LORD made Pharaoh's heart hard, so he chased the Israelites. The people of Israel looked up. There were the Egyptians marching after them! They were terrified and cried out to the LORD. They said to Moses, "Why did you bring us to the desert to die? What have you done to us?" Moses answered, "Don't be afraid. You'll see how the LORD will save you."

The LORD said to Moses, "Hold your wooden staff out over the Red Sea to part the water." Moses did so. All that night the LORD pushed the sea back with a strong east wind, and the people of Israel went through the sea on dry ground. There were walls of water on their right and left. But still the Egyptians followed them with their chariots and horses.

The LORD said, "Raise your hand over the sea again. The waters will rush back over the Egyptians." And so Moses raised his hand and the water rushed back. Not one of the Egyptians was left. The LORD had saved Israel from Egypt, so they put their trust in him. They were on their way back to the land God had promised to Abraham.

The Ten Commandments and the Law

(Exodus 13, 19, 24, 31–32, 34)

The LORD went ahead of the Israelites in a pillar of cloud. At night he led them with a pillar of fire. He led them near the place where Moses had seen the burning bush, to Mount Sinai.

The LORD called to Moses. "Tell the Israelites, 'You've seen what I did to the Egyptians. Now follow my laws fully. Keep my covenant, our agreement. If you do, out of all people, you'll be my special treasure.'"

The people got ready to hear from the LORD. On the third day Mount Sinai was covered in smoke because the LORD came down in a fire. The mountain shook. A trumpet sound grew louder and louder. Then the LORD said to Moses, "Come up to me on the mountain." The LORD wrote the Ten Commandments on two stone tablets and gave them to Moses. Moses stayed on the mountain 40 days and 40 nights.

The people didn't like waiting. So Aaron made them a calf of gold. They said, "Here's our god who brought us out of Egypt." And they bowed down to it.

God sent Moses back. When Moses saw the calf, he was furious. He burned it up.

God punished the people for their sin. But he did not forget his plan to take them to the Promised Land.

The Tabernacle

(Exodus 20–23, 25, 36, 40)

God gave the people of Israel laws for all areas of life to show them how to do right. Then the LORD said to Moses, "Tell the people to bring me an offering. Have them make a sacred tent for me. Then I'll live among them." He told Moses what they should bring and what to make.

The LORD had given certain workers the ability to make what was needed. They received from Moses all the offerings the people had brought. The people kept bringing the offerings

they'd chosen to give. So the skilled workers said to Moses, "The people are bringing more than enough for the work the LORD commanded us to do." So Moses stopped them from bringing more offerings.

When everything was ready, they set up the tent in the desert. It was called the Tent of Meeting or Tabernacle, and it had a large courtyard around it. Then the cloud of God covered the Tabernacle, and the glory of the LORD filled it. This cloud was above the holy tent every day. Fire was in the cloud at night. All the people of Israel could see the cloud during their travels.

The Twelve Spies

(Numbers 13–14)

The Israelites followed the cloud to Canaan, the land God had promised Abraham. Moses sent in twelve spies. After 40 days, they returned. They'd found bunches of grapes so big two men had to carry them!

Ten of them gave Moses this report: "We went into the country you sent us to. It really is a rich land! But the people who live there are too powerful."

Caleb, one of the other two spies, interrupted. "We should go in and take over. We can certainly do it."

But the men spoke again. "Everyone we saw was huge. We felt like grasshoppers beside them!"

Then all the Israelites moaned at Moses and Aaron, "If only we'd died in Egypt! Why has the Lord brought us here to die?"

Joshua and Caleb tore their clothes in anger. They told everyone, "We checked out the country. It's very good. If the Lord is pleased with us, he'll give it to us." But no one believed them.

God was very angry because the people didn't trust him. There were over 600,000 Israelite men aged 20 and older. But God said that of all these people only Joshua and Caleb would enter the land. And before this, the Israelites would wander for 40 years in the desert.

Joshua Leads Israel Across the Jordan

(Joshua 1, 3)

For 40 years the Israelites wandered in the desert. God looked after them and gave them all they needed. After this time, they took over part of the Promised Land, but the rest was on the other side of the Jordan River.

When Moses died, God spoke to Joshua, the new leader. He said, "Joshua, I'll be with you, just as I was with Moses. Now then, I want you and all these people to get ready to cross the river."

The priests prepared to carry the ark of the LORD. This was a huge wooden box covered in pure gold. Inside were the Ten Commandments, written on stone tablets.

The priests went ahead of the people. As soon as they stepped into the Jordan River, it stopped flowing. The water coming down the river piled up in one place a very long way off. The priests stood firm on dry ground in the middle of the river. They stayed there until the whole nation of Israel had gone across.

Into Jericho and Canaan

(Joshua 6, 10–11, 13–14)

After crossing the Jordan River, the Israelites came to the city of Jericho. The people of Jericho were terrified of them. The city gates were locked and guarded.

The LORD spoke to Joshua. He said, "I've handed over Jericho to you. March around the city once with your entire army. Do the same for six days. On the seventh day, march around the city seven times. Have seven priests blow trumpets of rams' horns as you march. You'll hear them blow a long blast on the horns. When

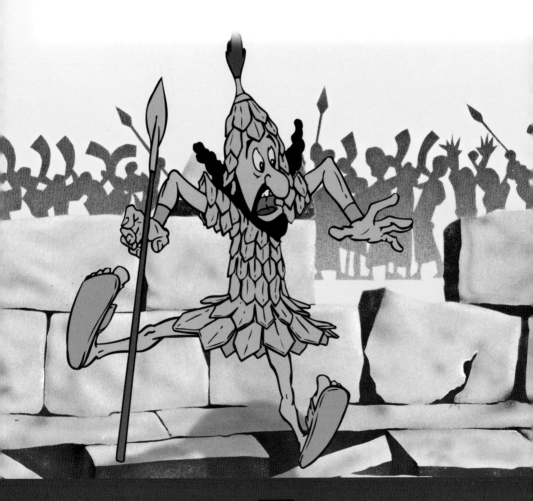

you do, tell all the men to give a loud shout. The walls of the city will fall down."

That's exactly what happened. When the walls fell down, the army rushed in and took over the city.

So Joshua and his men fought and won many battles. They brought a lot of the country under their control because God fought for Israel. He was fulfilling his promise to give the land to the family of Abraham. Joshua split up the land among the Israelites for them to live there. Then there was peace in the land.

Deborah Leads Israel

(Judges 2, 4)

Joshua lived to be 110 years old. But later on children were brought up without hearing about the great things the LORD had done for the Israelites. They deserted the LORD, the God of their forefathers, and did wicked things.

So God let their enemies beat them in battle. The nation of Israel suffered greatly. Then God gave them leaders called "judges." By listening to God, these leaders helped the army to win their battles. But when the judge died, the people returned to their evil ways. They worshiped other gods. This happened over and over and over again.

Deborah was one of those judges. People came to The Palm Tree of Deborah to ask her for advice. One day, God told her that the warrior Barak should gather an army. The LORD would give him power to beat Sisera, who was captain of the enemy army. "I'll only go if you go with me," Barak said. He trusted in people more than God.

"All right," Deborah replied, "I will. But you won't get any honor. The LORD will hand over Sisera to a woman instead."

As Barak's men marched out, the LORD drove back Sisera. His army was completely beaten. Sisera got out of his chariot and ran away. And a woman killed him, just as Deborah had said.

Samson

(Judges 13, 15–16)

Again the nation of Israel went back to their evil ways. So the LORD gave the Philistines power over them. The Philistines lived in Philistia, part of the Promised Land.

One day an Israelite woman saw an angel. "You'll have a son," he said. "He must never have his hair cut. He'll save Israel from the power of the Philistines."

When Samson was grown, he was very strong. The Philistines had him tied up. They were going to kill him. But the Spirit of the LORD came on Samson with power. The ropes on him became like burned thread and dropped off. Samson grabbed a donkey's jawbone and killed 1,000 Philistines with it!

Samson's girlfriend was called Delilah. In return for a lot of money, she told the Philistines to cut Samson's hair. They did. Then God's strength left him, so they took him prisoner. Thousands of Philistines came to a party in their temple. They brought in Samson to laugh at him.

Samson prayed, "God, please make me strong just once more." Then he pushed with all his might against the two pillars that held up the temple.

The building fell down and many people died! That day, the Israelites knew who the true God was.

Ruth

(Ruth 1, 3–4)

In the time of the judges, there came a famine in Israel. There was no food.

So a man moved with his family to another country. When he and his sons died, his wife, Naomi, set out to return to Israel.

The two women who had married her sons were now widows. One of them decided to go home to her mother and her country's gods. But the other, Ruth, said, "Don't ask me to leave you. Where you go, I'll go. Your people will be my people. Your God will be my God." So they went to live in Bethlehem.

Ruth started working in the fields of a man called Boaz. It turned out that Boaz was Naomi's close relative. Boaz liked Ruth. He cared for her and made sure she and Naomi had food.

In those days a widow's closest relative looked after the widow by marrying her. Boaz said to Ruth, "Don't be afraid. There's another man more closely related to you than I am. If he wants to help you, good. But if he doesn't, then I will."

The other man already had a family. So Boaz married Ruth. This was all part of God's plan.

Samuel

(1 Samuel 1, 3, 7)

Hannah couldn't have children. She was very sad. So she promised that if God gave her a son, she'd give him back to God. He would serve the LORD all the days of his life. Soon afterwards she had a baby, Samuel. When he was still very little, Hannah took Samuel to the priest, Eli, so he could live in the temple.

She said, "The LORD has given me what I asked him for. So now I'm giving this child to the LORD."

Eli brought up Samuel and taught him to serve the LORD.

One night the LORD called out to Samuel. Samuel ran to Eli. He said, "Here I am. You called me." But Eli said, "I didn't call you. Go back to bed." This happened three times. Then Eli told Samuel, "Go and lie down. If someone calls out to you again, say, 'Speak, LORD. I'm listening.'"

Samuel did as Eli said. God gave him a message. That was the beginning of Samuel's life as a judge and servant of God. As Samuel grew up, the LORD was with him. Samuel spoke for God, and everything he said came true.

Samuel led Israel all the days of his life. He was Israel's last judge.

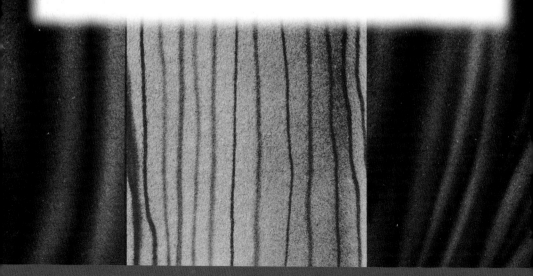

King Saul
(1 Samuel 8, 10, 13)

When Samuel was old, the Israelites asked for a king instead of another judge.

The LORD told Samuel, "Let them have what they want. But warn them strongly."

So Samuel warned them: "The king who rules over you will fight wars, make your children serve him, and take your land. You'll be his slaves." But the people wanted to be like all the other nations.

God chose a man named Saul. But when the Israelites gathered to make him king, he couldn't be found. The LORD said to Samuel, "He has hidden among the baggage." So they ran over there and brought him out.

Then the people shouted, "Long live the king!"

The years passed. King Saul was losing a war. Samuel got a message from God. He told Saul to wait for him. Samuel would burn an offering to God for Saul. Only priests were allowed to do this. But Saul's army began to run away from the battle. So King Saul offered the sacrifice himself. Just as he finished, Samuel arrived. "You have done a foolish thing," he said. "You haven't done as God told you. You won't be king much longer. In fact, the LORD has already chosen a new leader, a man who is close to his heart."

David and Goliath

(1 Samuel 17–18)

While Saul was still king, Israel was at war with the Philistines. The Philistines had a soldier called Goliath. He was as tall as a giant. Every day for 40 days he came out of their camp and shouted for someone to fight him.

David was a young shepherd from Bethlehem. He knew the God of Israel would help him beat Goliath, so he stepped forward. King Saul offered him his own armor. But David took his shepherd's staff and sling instead. The sling could be used to throw stones a long way.

When Goliath saw how young David was, he hated him. He said, "Why are you coming at me with a stick? Do you think I'm a dog? Come over here!"

David said, "You're coming to fight me with a sword and a spear. But I'm coming against you in the name of the LORD. Today the whole world will know God is with Israel."

As Goliath moved closer, David took out a stone. He put it in his sling. He slung it at Goliath. The stone hit him on the forehead. Goliath fell face down.

When the Philistines saw that their hero was dead, they turned and ran away.

After that, David became very popular. The people loved him. But King Saul became jealous of him.

David and Jonathan

(1 Samuel 18, 20, 23)

Jonathan was King Saul's son. He and David became close friends. Jonathan made a covenant, a special agreement, with David because he loved him as much as he loved himself. To show this, he took off his robe and gave it to David. He even gave him his sword, his bow, and his belt.

One day King Saul threw a spear at David because he was jealous of him. David asked Jonathan to find out if Saul wanted to kill him. They agreed on a signal. David would hide in a field. If Saul wanted to kill David, Jonathan would shoot his arrows far out into the field. If Jonathan shot only a little way into the field, David was safe.

The next morning Jonathan shot arrows far into the field. David came out of hiding. The two friends hugged each other goodbye. They were very sad.

Jonathan said, "Go in peace. In the name of the LORD we've made an unbreakable promise. We've promised that we and our families will be friends forever."

Jonathan knew that someday David would be king instead of his father.

David Becomes King

(1 Samuel 16, 31; 2 Samuel 1, 5, 9)

After Saul had turned away from him, God looked for a new man to lead Israel. He found David, a shepherd boy who was faithfully caring for his father's sheep. He sent the prophet Samuel to him. God said to Samuel, "I don't look at the things people look at. I see what's in someone's heart." Although David had seven older brothers, Samuel knew he had to pour the special anointing oil over David. This was the sign for a chosen king.

There were many difficult times ahead of David. King Saul was against him, but God was with him. David was a man close to God's heart.

Finally, King Saul killed himself during a battle because he was terrified of the Philistines. David's covenant friend, Jonathan, was fighting with his father. He also died. David wrote a song for them because he was so sad.

David ruled over all Israel at last. He remembered his promise to Jonathan. There was a son of Jonathan who couldn't walk. So David ordered that he should live in the palace and eat the king's food for the rest of his days.

Introduction to Psalms— Psalm 1

David and others wrote of their love for God in poems and songs called psalms. Some psalms focus on God and his actions. Some are for us to praise and worship God together. They tell him of our love and longing to follow him. Some psalms thank God for who he is and what he does. Others just tell God how we feel—happy, sad, worried, or confused.

Psalm 1 says people who live God's way are blessed. God watches over them.

Blessed are those who don't follow the
     advice of wicked people.
   They don't do what sinners do.
They don't join those who make fun of the
     LORD and his law.
   Instead, they find joy in doing everything
     the LORD wants.
They think about his law day and night.
   They're like trees that are planted along
     the riverbank.
They always bear fruit when they should.
   Their leaves don't dry up.
Everything godly people do turns out well.
   But this is not true of wicked people.
They are like useless chaff, which the wind
     blows away.
   They will not stand upright when God
     judges them.
Sinners will have no place among the godly.
   For the LORD watches over those who are
     godly.
But the lives of wicked people will lead to
     their death.

Psalm 23—The Shepherd's Psalm

David knew that God loves and takes care of his people. In Psalm 23 David tells how God guides us and protects us through whatever happens in life.

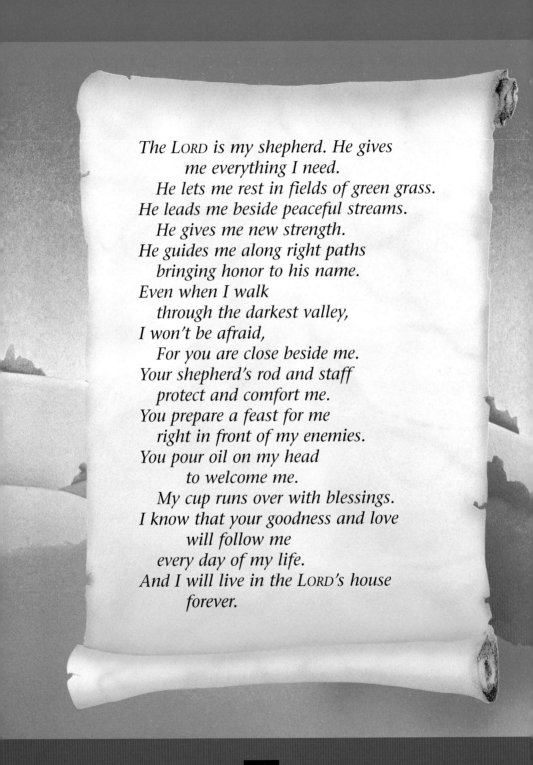

The Lord is my shepherd. He gives
*   me everything I need.*
* He lets me rest in fields of green grass.*
He leads me beside peaceful streams.
* He gives me new strength.*
He guides me along right paths
*   bringing honor to his name.*
Even when I walk
*   through the darkest valley,*
I won't be afraid,
*   For you are close beside me.*
Your shepherd's rod and staff
*   protect and comfort me.*
You prepare a feast for me
*   right in front of my enemies.*
You pour oil on my head
*   to welcome me.*
* My cup runs over with blessings.*
I know that your goodness and love
*   will follow me*
* every day of my life.*
And I will live in the Lord's house
*   forever.*

Psalm 150—A Praise Psalm

Psalm 150 is a celebration song. Everyone shouts out how good God is, making music with whatever they can get their hands on. It's like being at a party!

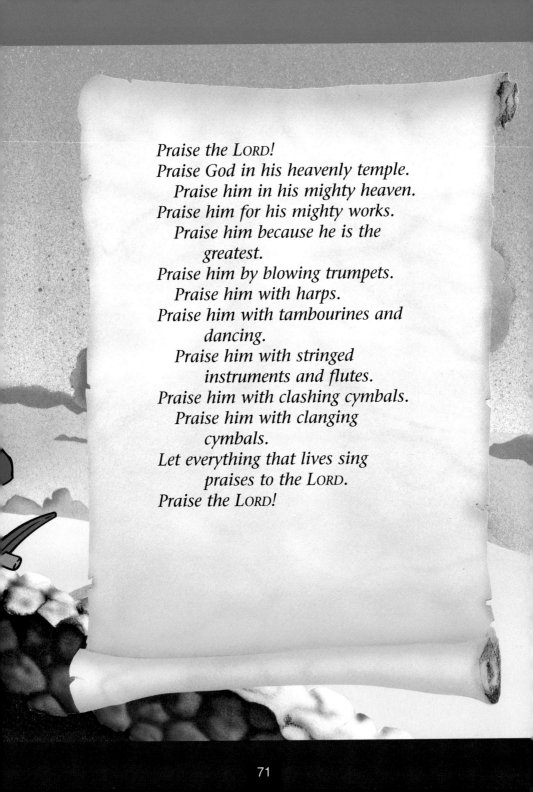

Praise the L<small>ORD</small>!
Praise God in his heavenly temple.
   Praise him in his mighty heaven.
Praise him for his mighty works.
   Praise him because he is the
      greatest.
Praise him by blowing trumpets.
   Praise him with harps.
Praise him with tambourines and
      dancing.
   Praise him with stringed
      instruments and flutes.
Praise him with clashing cymbals.
   Praise him with clanging
      cymbals.
Let everything that lives sing
      praises to the L<small>ORD</small>.
Praise the L<small>ORD</small>!

Solomon, His Wisdom and Wealth

(1 Kings 2–4)

David ruled over all Israel for 33 years. His family was important in God's plan. When he was old he told his son Solomon, "Do everything the LORD your God has commanded. If you do this, God will keep the promise he made to me: 'Your sons must be faithful to me with all their heart and soul. Then your family will always rule over Israel.'"

After Solomon became king, God spoke to him in a dream. "Ask for anything you want," he said.

Solomon answered, "I don't know how to carry out my duties. So please give me a mind that understands. Then I'll be able to tell the difference between what's right and what's wrong."

The LORD was pleased. So God said to him, "Because that's what you've asked for and not long life or money and things for yourself, I'll do what you ask. And that's not all. I'll give you riches, and your people will honor you. As long as you live, no other king will be as great as you'll be. And if you do what my law commands, just as your father David did, I'll give you a long life."

God made Solomon very wise. Kings everywhere heard how wise Solomon was. So they sent their people to listen to him.

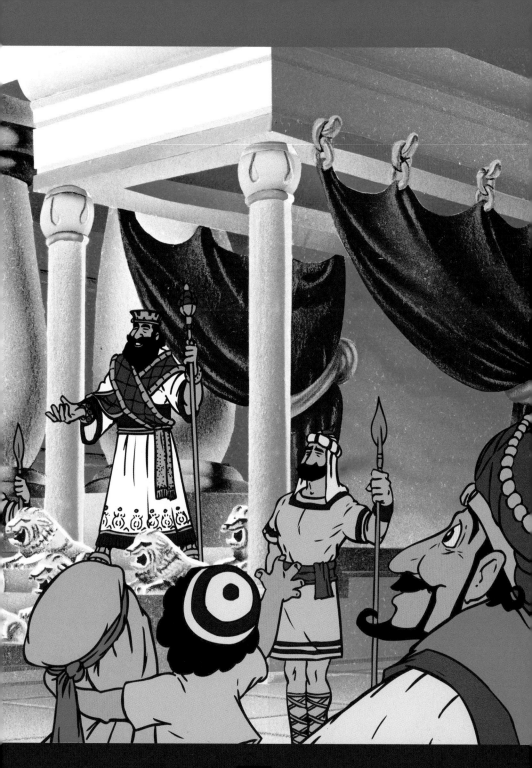

Solomon Builds the Temple

(2 Chronicles 3, 5–7)

All this time the Israelites still came to the Tabernacle, the tent they'd made in the desert, to meet with God. But King Solomon built a stone temple for God in Jerusalem, the capital city. He covered the inside with pure gold. He decorated it with precious jewels.

When it was finished, the whole nation of Israel came together for two weeks. Men from Aaron's family line served God as priests. They put the ark of God's covenant inside the temple and sacrificed many offerings to the LORD. The trumpet players and singers made music together. They sang, "He is good. His faithful love continues forever."

Solomon said, "LORD, you're the God of Israel. There's no God like you in heaven or on earth. You keep your promises. You show us your love when we obey you and are eager to do your will. But will you really live on earth with human beings? Even the highest heavens can't hold you! My God, listen to the prayers offered in this place."

As Solomon finished praying, fire came down from heaven. It burned up the burnt offering and the sacrifices. And God's presence filled the temple. Then the Israelites celebrated and were very glad.

Proverbs

(Proverbs 1–2, 10, 12, 17)

Solomon wrote many sayings called proverbs. They teach us to be wise, which means that we choose the best way to live. He said:

"Be wise: If you really want to know a lot, you'll begin by first having respect for the LORD. A wise heart listens to commands. Imagine how you'd look for some silver or hidden treasure. You'd look really hard. Search for the ability to be wise the same way.

"Work hard and listen to advice: Hands that work hard will be put in charge. But people who don't want to work will become

slaves. Foolish people think they're perfect. But wise people listen to advice.

"Be careful what you say: Thoughtless words cut like a sword. But the words of wise people bring healing. The LORD hates lips that tell lies. But he's pleased with people who tell the truth.

"Be a good friend: If someone upsets you, forgive and forget. That builds love. Friends love at all times. They're there to help when trouble comes."

The Nation Splits

(1 Kings 11–12)

Unfortunately, King Solomon didn't always act wisely himself. He married many women from nations that served other gods. As he grew old, he began to worship their gods, too.

The LORD became angry. He said he'd tear away the kingdom from Solomon's son, Rehoboam. "But," he said, "he'll still rule over one of the tribes because of my servant David." (The twelve tribes of Israel were the families of Jacob's twelve sons.)

Rehoboam became the next king. An important man called Jeroboam and all the Israelites came to him. They said, "Make our

hard work easier. Then we'll serve you." The older men who had been King Solomon's advisers agreed with them. But the king didn't listen to them or the people. Instead, he listened to the young men who were his own advisers. The LORD had planned it that way. Rehoboam answered the Israelites, "My father put a heavy load on your shoulders. But I'll make it even heavier."

Then all of the people of Israel said, "Who cares about David's royal family? Let them look after themselves!" So Israel made Jeroboam their king instead.

Only the tribe of Judah stayed with David's family. So the kingdom was divided in two: Israel and Judah.

Elijah, Prophet to Israel

(1 Kings 16, 18)

King Jeroboam and the Israelite kings after him served other gods, like the god Baal. But God sent messengers, also known as prophets, to call the people back to him.

The prophet Elijah gathered the Israelites and Baal's prophets on a mountaintop. "If the LORD is the one and only God, follow him. But if Baal is God, follow him," he cried.

Elijah and Baal's prophets prepared bulls to sacrifice. Elijah said, "You pray to your god. And I'll pray to the LORD. The god who answers by sending down fire is the one and only God."

Baal's prophets prayed all day.

"Shout louder!" Elijah cried. "Perhaps Baal has too much to think about. Or maybe he's away on a trip!" So they shouted louder until they were half crazy. But no one answered.

Elijah poured twelve huge pots of water over his altar. Then he prayed, "LORD, answer me. Then these people will know that you're God."

Straight away, the fire of the LORD came down. It burned up the sacrifice, the wood, the stones, and the soil on the ground. It even licked up the water in the ditch! When all the people saw it, they cried out, "The LORD is the one and only God!"

Jonah and the Huge Fish

(Jonah 1–3)

God cared about other nations, too. He told a prophet, Jonah, to preach to the city of Nineveh.

Jonah didn't want to go, so he ran away and got on a ship. But a wild storm came up on the Mediterranean Sea. It was so wild that the ship was in danger of breaking apart.

The sailors found out Jonah was running away from the LORD. They became terrified. They asked Jonah, "What should we do to make the sea calm down?"

"Throw me into it," he replied. "It's my fault this terrible storm has come on you." Then they threw Jonah overboard. And the rough sea became calm.

But the LORD sent a huge fish to swallow Jonah. Jonah was inside the fish for three days and three nights. Inside the fish Jonah prayed to the LORD his God. Then the LORD spoke to the fish and it spat Jonah up onto dry land.

So Jonah preached to Nineveh. He announced, "In 40 days Nineveh will be destroyed." The people of Nineveh believed God's warning. God saw that they stopped doing what was evil, so he took pity on them. He didn't destroy them as he'd said he would.

Israel's Rebellion

(2 Kings 17)

Nineveh turned to God, but the Israelites didn't. God wanted his people to follow him from their hearts, not just with words. But the Israelites kept acting wickedly. So God warned them that because of their sin an enemy would beat them in war and take them away from the land of Israel.

The Lord spoke to the Israelites through his prophets again and again. He said, "Turn from your evil ways. Obey my commands and laws." But the people wouldn't listen. They didn't believe in the Lord. They didn't pay any attention to the warnings. They bowed down to the sun, moon, and stars and worshiped statues of Baal and other worthless gods. They turned to fortune-tellers. They copied the nations around them. They did exactly what the Lord had told them not to do.

Finally, the Lord turned his back on them. God's warnings came true. The king of Assyria marched into the land of Israel. He took away all those living in Israel. He sent them off to the land of Assyria. Then he brought in other people to live in Israel.

Isaiah and Jeremiah, Prophets to Judah

(Isaiah 1, 5, 7; Jeremiah 25, 31)

God had warned those who lived in Israel. He also warned the tribe of Judah through prophets like Isaiah and Jeremiah: "You must be willing to change and do what I command. Watch out all you who say what's evil is good and what's good is evil."

The prophets told the people of Judah that if they kept sinning, the king of Babylon would destroy Jerusalem and the temple and take them prisoner for 70 years.

But there was a future and a hope for the family of David.

Through the prophets God also said, "My love for you is a love that lasts forever.

"The LORD himself will give you a special sign. By a miracle, a virgin will give birth to a son. And he'll be called Immanuel. (Immanuel means "God is with us.")

"Even though your sins are now bright red, they'll be as white as snow."

He promised, "I'll put my law in your minds and write it on your hearts. I'll be your God. And you'll be my people."

So the Israelites knew that a special king would come into the family of David one day.

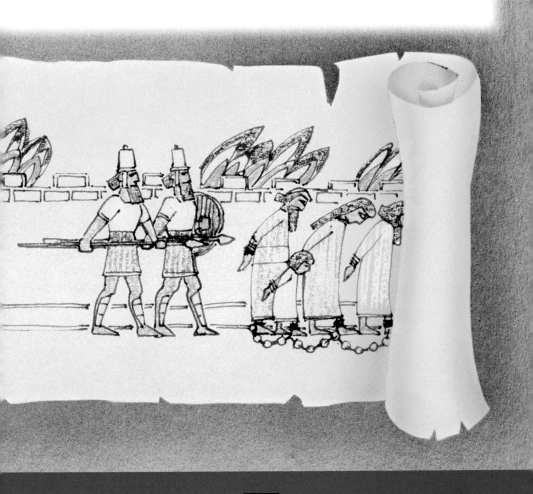

The Exile

(2 Kings 25)

The people of Judah didn't listen to the prophets. Some years later everything happened as the prophets had said.

Nebuchadnezzar, king of Babylon, marched out against Jerusalem with all his armies. He set up camp outside the city. He put up ladders and built ramps and war towers all around. He kept the people trapped inside Jerusalem.

After two years, there wasn't any food left in the city. So the people didn't have anything to eat. Then part of the city wall was broken down. Judah's whole army ran away at night. But the armies of Babylon chased the king of Judah. They caught up with him on the plains of Jericho, for by then his men had all left him.

The Babylonians set the LORD's holy temple on fire. Everything inside was broken up or taken to Babylon. They also set fire to the royal palace and all the houses in Jerusalem. They burned down every important building. The armies of Babylon even broke down the walls around Jerusalem.

The king and the people of Judah were taken prisoner. They were taken far away from their own land, just as God had said.

Daniel and Friends

(Daniel 1)

At the king's palace in Babylon some prisoners were picked out to train for three years. They'd serve the king. Among these were Daniel and his three friends.

The king had his servants give these men food and wine from his own table. But God had given his people strict rules about eating, so Daniel wouldn't eat the king's food.

The chief official, the man in charge, said, "I'm afraid of the king. Why should he see you looking worse than the others?"

So Daniel said to his guard, "Please test us for ten days. Give us nothing but vegetables to eat and water to drink. Then compare us with the young men who eat the king's food." So he tested them for ten days. After the ten days they looked healthy and well fed. In fact, they looked even better than the others. So from then on, the guard gave them only vegetables and water.

God allowed these four young men to know and understand many things. They understood all sorts of subjects and writings. And Daniel could understand visions and dreams of all kinds. The king saw that no one else was like them. Their answers were always the best.

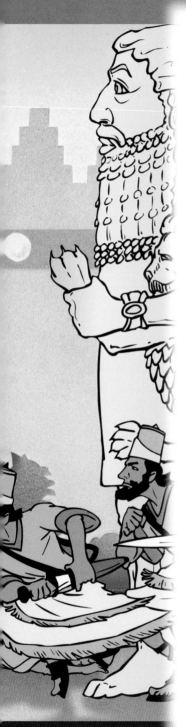

The Blazing Oven

(Daniel 3)

Daniel and his friends became important men in the kingdom of Babylon.

Later, the king made a huge gold statue for everyone to bow down to. Daniel's friends refused. The king said, "Worship the statue I made. If you don't, you'll be thrown at once into a huge, blazing oven. Then what god will be able to save you from my powerful hand?"

The friends replied, "The God we serve is able to bring us out alive. But even if he doesn't, Your Majesty, we still won't serve your gods or worship the gold statue you set up."

The king was furious! He made the oven seven times hotter than usual and had Daniel's three friends thrown in.

Then King Nebuchadnezzar leaped to his feet. He asked his advisers, "Didn't we throw three men into the fire? Look! I see four men walking around. They aren't even hurt by the flames! And the fourth man looks like a son of the gods!"

He told the friends to come out of the oven. They were fine. Their clothes didn't even smell of smoke! The king was so amazed, he made a law. Anyone who said anything against the God of these three friends would be punished.

Daniel and the Lions' Den

(Daniel 5–6)

Years later there was a new king in Babylon. Daniel was the third highest ruler in the kingdom. Other leaders were jealous. They tried to find fault with Daniel's work. But they couldn't. So they had a royal law made: Whoever prayed to anyone except the king would be thrown into the lions' den. But Daniel kept praying to God.

When the king heard about it, he tried to save Daniel. But the royal law couldn't be changed, so Daniel was thrown into the lions' den. The king said, "You always serve your God faithfully. May he save you!"

As soon as the sun began to rise, the king got up. He hurried to the lions' pit. As soon as he got near, he called out to Daniel, "Daniel! You serve the living God faithfully. Has he been able to save you from the lions?"

Daniel answered from out of the pit, "My king, may you live forever! My God sent his angel to shut the lions' mouths because I haven't done anything wrong. They haven't hurt me at all."

The king was very happy. He ordered his servants to lift Daniel out of the den. They didn't see any wounds or marks on him. Why not? Because he had trusted his God.

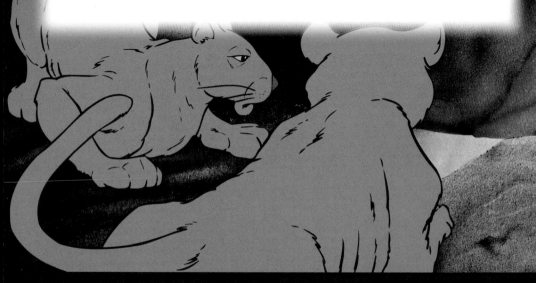

Esther

(Esther 2–5, 7–8)

Esther, a beautiful Jewish girl, became queen in Babylon. A time came when the king commanded everyone to kneel down and praise an important man called Haman. The queen's cousin, Mordecai, refused. Haman was furious. He had a law passed ordering all the Jews (or Israelites) in the kingdom to be killed. So Mordecai begged Queen Esther to help them.

She said, "I'll have to go to the king in the inner courtyard without being sent for. The law says anyone who does this must die. But if the king reaches out his gold rod toward me, my life will

be saved. So let all the Jews pray for me and not eat for three days and nights."

Esther went to see the king. He held out the gold rod! So Esther invited him and Haman to two royal parties. At the second one the king asked, "What do you want, Queen Esther?"

Queen Esther answered, "Your Majesty, please let me and my people live." She told him about Haman's plan to kill the Jews.

The king was very angry. He had Haman killed instead. Then he wrote another law that saved the Jews. God had used Esther to save his people!

The Return

(Ezra 5–6; Nehemiah 4, 6, 8, 10)

God had promised his people, Israel, that they would return to their land.

The people returned in groups over many years. Important men led each group of people.

Zerubbabel and Jeshua began to rebuild God's temple. The prophets of God were with them and helped them. The people finished building. Then they met together to present the temple to the LORD. They celebrated with great joy.

Then Nehemiah helped the people rebuild Jerusalem's walls. Their enemies tried hard to stop them. So those who brought what the builders needed worked with one hand. In the other they held a weapon. Each builder wore his sword at his side.

When everything was completed, Ezra, a priest and teacher, read from God's holy book. He read the Law to them from sunrise until the middle of the day. And all the people paid full attention. They promised to follow the Law of God and to keep carefully all the commands, rules, and laws of the LORD.

So God's people came back to the Promised Land.

Mary and Joseph

(Matthew 1; Luke 1)

Long ago, God had promised Abraham, Isaac, Jacob, and David that one from their family line would make people right with God. Now it was finally time.

He sent the angel Gabriel to a virgin named Mary. The angel said, "God is very pleased with you, Mary. You will have a son, and you are to name him Jesus. The power of the Most High God will cover you. So the baby born to you will be holy, and he will be called the Son of God."

Mary had promised to marry Joseph, a carpenter. But before they were married Mary became pregnant by the power of God. Joseph was a godly man. He didn't know about the angel's message. He decided to quietly break off his plans to marry Mary.

As he was thinking about this, an angel came to him in a dream. The angel said, "Don't be afraid to take Mary home as your wife. The baby inside her is from the Holy Spirit. She's going to have a son. Give him the name Jesus because he'll save his people from their sins." When Joseph woke up, he did what the angel had commanded and married Mary.

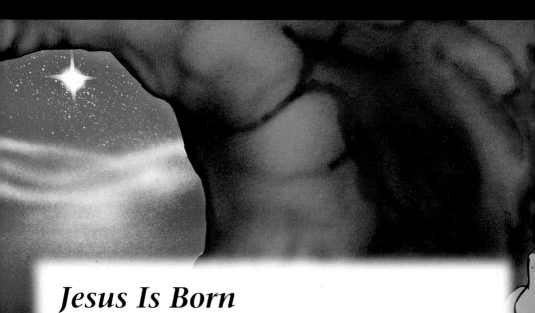

Jesus Is Born

(Matthew 1; Luke 2)

In those days, the Romans ruled over the land of Israel. Their leader, the emperor Augustus, decided to make a list of everybody who lived under his control. So everyone went to their hometowns to be listed.

Joseph and Mary—who was almost ready to have her baby—went too. They went to Bethlehem, David's town, because Joseph belonged to David's family line.

Bethlehem was so busy because of the emperor's law that there was no room for Mary and Joseph at any guest house or inn.

While they were there, the time came for the child to be born. Mary gave birth to her first baby, a boy. She wrapped him in large pieces of cloth. Then she placed him in a wooden box, which held food for horses, donkeys, and cows—a manger. Joseph and Mary named the baby Jesus. The angel had given this name before his mother became pregnant. Jesus was also called "Immanuel" meaning "God is with us" because he was God's Son.

It all happened as the angel had said it would.

Angels Come to See Some Shepherds

(Luke 2)

Shepherds used to look after their sheep in the hills near Bethlehem. One night they suddenly saw an angel of the Lord. And the Lord's glory shone around them. They were terrified.

But the angel said to them, "Don't be afraid. I bring you good news of great joy. It's for everyone. Today in David's town a Savior has been born for you. He is the Messiah, the Lord. You'll know it's him when you find a baby wrapped in cloth and lying in a manger."

Suddenly many more angels appeared, praising God. They said, "Let glory come to God in the highest heaven! And may peace come to those he's pleased with on earth!"

The angels left and went into heaven. Then the shepherds said to one another, "Let's go to Bethlehem. Let's see this thing that's happened." They hurried to find Mary and Joseph and the baby. The baby was lying in a manger. After seeing him, they told everyone what the angel had said about this child. All who heard it were amazed.

But Mary treasured all these things in her heart. She often thought about them.

The Wise Men

(Matthew 2)

Some wise men who studied the stars came to Jerusalem. They were following an unusual star. They believed the star was a sign that a special king had been born. They went to the palace and asked, "Where is the child who's been born to be king of the Jews?"

When King Herod heard this, he was very upset. He wanted to be the only king. He called the chief priests and the teachers of the law. He asked them where the Messiah (or Christ) was to be born. (The Jews knew about God's plan to send a man to make things right between people and God. "The Messiah" is a name for that special person.)

"In Bethlehem in Judea," they replied.

Herod said to the wise men, "As soon as you find him, tell me. I'll worship him too."

The wise men left. The star stopped over the place where the child was. The wise men saw the child with his mother Mary. They bowed down and worshiped him. They gave him gold, incense, and myrrh.

But God warned them in a dream not to go back to Herod. So they went home another way.

When the wise men had gone, Joseph had a dream. An angel came to him. "Get up!" the angel said. "Take the child and his mother and escape to Egypt. Stay there until I tell you to come back. Herod wants to kill the child." So they left for Egypt in the middle of the night. They did not return until Herod had died.

The Boy Jesus at the Temple

(Luke 2)

When they came back from Egypt, Jesus' family lived in a town called Nazareth.

Every year Jesus' parents went to Jerusalem for the Passover celebration. When he was 12 years old, they went up to Jerusalem as usual. Afterward, his parents left with a big group of others to go back home. Jesus stayed behind, but they didn't know.

That night they looked for him among their relatives and friends. He wasn't there. So they went back to Jerusalem. After three days they found Jesus in the temple. He was sitting with the teachers, discussing difficult questions with them. Everyone who heard him was amazed at how much he understood and at his answers.

When his parents saw him, his mother said, "Son, why have you done this to us? Your father and I have been worried. We've been looking for you everywhere."

"Why were you looking for me?" he asked. "Didn't you know I had to be in my Father's house?" But they didn't understand what he meant.

He went back to Nazareth with them and was obedient to them. And Jesus became wiser and stronger. He pleased God and people more and more.

Jesus Is Baptized
(Matthew 3; Mark 1; Luke 3)

Jesus' cousin, John, preached in the desert. He said to the crowds who came to listen, "The kingdom of heaven is near. Turn from your sins and turn to God to be forgiven." Those who did were baptized in the Jordan River.

John's clothes were made of camel's hair. He had a leather belt around his waist. His food was grasshoppers and wild honey.

When Jesus was about 30 years old, he came to the river. He wanted to be baptized by John. But John told Jesus, "I need to be baptized by you. So why have you come to me?"

Jesus replied, "Let it be this way for now. It's right for us to do this. It's part of God's holy plan." Then John agreed.

Jesus was baptized and came out of the water. At that moment heaven was opened. Jesus saw God's Spirit coming down on him like a dove. A voice spoke from heaven. It said, "You're my Son, and I love you. I'm very pleased with you."

This was the beginning of Jesus' work.

Jesus Is Tempted

(Matthew 4; Luke 4)

The Holy Spirit led Jesus into the desert.
There the devil tempted him. After 40
days and nights without eating, Jesus
was hungry. The tempter said, "If you're
the Son of God, change these stones
into bread."

Jesus answered, "It says in God's holy
book, 'People don't live only on bread.
They live on every word that comes from
God's mouth.'"

Then the devil took Jesus to the
highest point of the temple. "If you're
the Son of God," he said, "jump off! It
says in God's book, 'The Lord will
command his angels to protect you.
They'll lift you up in their hands, to keep
you from hitting your feet on a stone.'"

Jesus answered, "It also says, 'Do not
test the Lord your God.'"

Finally, the devil took Jesus to a very
high mountain. He showed him all the
kingdoms of the world and how
marvellous they were. "If you bow
down and worship me," he said, "I'll
give you all this."

Jesus said, "Get away from me, Satan!
God's book says, 'Worship the Lord your
God. Serve only him.'"

Then the devil went away, and angels
came and took care of Jesus.

The Twelve Disciples

(Matthew 10; Mark 1, 3; Luke 6)

After his temptation in the desert, Jesus returned to the area called Galilee.

One day Jesus was walking beside a lake called the Sea of Galilee. He saw Simon and his brother Andrew. They were fishermen. "Come. Follow me," Jesus said. "I will show you how to fish for people." At once, they left their nets and followed him.

Jesus walked a little farther. He saw James and John, the sons of Zebedee. They were in a boat mending their nets. He called out to them. Right away, they left their father, Zebedee, in the boat and followed Jesus.

Later on, Jesus went to a mountainside to pray. He spent the night praying. When morning came, he called together his disciples. He chose twelve to be with him. They'd be the first he'd send out to preach and to heal the sick.

Simon was one of the disciples. Jesus gave him the name Peter. There were also Simon's brother Andrew, James, John, Philip, and Bartholomew. And there were Matthew, Thomas, and James, who was the son of Alphaeus. Simon nicknamed the Zealot and Judas were also Jesus' disciples. Another Judas, Judas Iscariot, was one of them too. He was the one who would later hand over Jesus to those who wanted to kill him.

Jesus the Miracle Worker

(Matthew 14; John 6)

One day, a crowd of about 5,000 men, plus women and children, was with Jesus, listening to him teach about God. To test the disciples, Jesus asked them how they would feed the people. Philip answered, "We could never afford to buy enough bread!"

Andrew said, "Here's a boy with five small loaves of bread and two small fish. But how far will that go in such a large crowd?"

Jesus had all the people sit down in groups. Then Jesus took the loaves and gave thanks. The disciples handed them out. Then he did the same with the fish. There was more than enough for everyone to eat, and the disciples filled twelve baskets with what was left over!

Later that night Jesus made the disciples get into a boat and head across the lake without him. It was dark. A strong wind was blowing, and the water became rough. Then they saw Jesus coming toward the boat, walking on the water. They were terrified.

But he said, "I am here. Don't be afraid."

When he climbed into the boat, the wind died down. Then the disciples worshiped him. They said, "You really are the Son of God!"

Jesus the Healer

(Matthew 4, 9; Luke 18)

Jesus showed people God loved them by healing them. People brought everyone who wasn't well to him. Some were in great pain. Some couldn't walk, and others couldn't move at all. Jesus healed all of them.

One day a blind man begging by the road to Jericho heard that Jesus was walking by. So he called out, "Jesus! Have mercy on me!" The people told him to be quiet, but he shouted louder.

Jesus stopped. "What do you want?" he asked.

"Lord, I want to be able to see."

Jesus said, "Receive your sight. Your faith has healed you." Right away he could see. He followed Jesus, giving God praise. All the people praised God too.

Another time, a well-known man knelt down in front of Jesus. He said, "My daughter has just died. But come and place your hand on her. Then she'll come back to life."

Jesus went with him. When Jesus entered the man's house, he saw the noisy crowd and heard the funeral music. He said, "Go away. The girl isn't dead. She's asleep." But they laughed at him.

After the crowd had been sent outside, Jesus went in. He took the girl by the hand, and she got up! She was alive!

Jesus the Teacher

(Matthew 5, 7)

Jesus went up on a mountainside with his disciples. He began to teach them:

"Those who know they need God are blessed. The kingdom of heaven belongs to them. Those who are deeply sad are blessed. They'll be comforted. Those who are free from pride are blessed. They'll be given the whole earth. Those who are hungry and thirsty for what's right are blessed. They'll be filled. Those who show mercy are blessed. Mercy will be shown to them. Those whose hearts are pure are blessed. They'll see God. Those who make peace are blessed. They'll be called children of God. Those who suffer for doing right are blessed. The kingdom of heaven belongs to them.

"You're the light of the world. Let your light shine in front of others so they can see the good things you do and praise your Father in heaven.

"Love your enemies. Pray for those who hurt you.

"Don't judge others. Then you won't be judged.

"Do for others what you would like them to do for you. This sums up what the Law and the prophets teach."

Introduction to Parables—The Wise Builder

(Matthew 7, 13; Luke 8)

Jesus taught using stories called parables. He didn't say anything to the crowds without telling a story. And so what God had promised long ago through a prophet came true. God had said, "I'll speak to you in parables. I'll tell about things that have been hidden since the world was made."

Isaiah, too, had declared, "They see, but they don't know what they're seeing. They hear, but they don't understand." This meant that those who wanted to understand Jesus' stories and teaching would understand. But those who didn't would just hear a story.

Jesus said, "Everyone who hears my words and obeys them is like a wise man who built his house on the rock. The rain came down. The water rose. The winds beat against that house. But it didn't fall. It was built on the rock.

"But everyone who hears my words and doesn't obey them is like a foolish man who built his house on sand. The rain came down. The water rose. The winds beat against that house. And it fell with a loud crash."

Parables—The Good Samaritan

(Luke 10; John 4)

One day a man who knew God's laws very well tried to test Jesus. He asked, "What must I do to be saved?" Jesus told him to love God with all his heart, soul, and mind. He was also to love his neighbor as himself.

The man asked, "Who's my neighbor?"

Jesus replied, "A man was going from Jerusalem to Jericho. Robbers attacked him. They stripped him and beat him, leaving him almost dead. A priest was going down that same road. When he saw the man, he passed by on the other side. A temple worker also came by and did the same.

"But then someone from Samaria came past." (Jews didn't have anything to do with Samaritans.) "When he saw the man, he felt sorry for him. He went to him and bandaged his wounds. Then he brought the man to a guest house and took care of him. The next day he gave some money to the owner of the guest house. 'Take care of him,' he said. 'When I come back, I'll pay you for anything extra.'

"Which of the three was a neighbor to the man attacked by robbers?"

The man replied, "The one who helped him."

Jesus told him, "Go and do as he did."

Parables—The Seeds

(Luke 8)

Jesus told the crowds this story:

He said, "A farmer went out to sow his seed. As he sowed, some fell on a footpath. People walked on it, and the birds ate it up. Some fell on rocky ground. When it grew, the plants dried up because they had no water. Other seed fell among thorns. The thorns crowded out the good plants. Still other seed fell on good soil. It produced a harvest 100 times more than the farmer planted."

Jesus' disciples asked what the story meant.

He replied, "The seed is God's message. The seed that fell on the footpath is like those who hear. But the devil takes the message from their hearts so they won't believe. The seed that fell on rocky ground is like those who hear the message and receive it with joy. But they have no deep roots. When they are tested, they fall away from the faith. The seed among thorns stands for those who hear the message, but the worries, riches, and pleasures in life crowd it out. They don't reach full growth.

"But the seed on good soil stands for those who have an honest heart. They hear the message and keep it in their hearts. They remain faithful and produce a good harvest.

"So be careful how you listen."

Prayer

(Matthew 6–7; Luke 11)

Jesus taught people how to pray. He said, "Your Father knows what you need even before you ask him.

"Ask, then you'll get. Search, then you'll find. Knock, then the door will be opened. All who ask will receive. All who search will find. And the door will be opened to all who knock.

"You parents, suppose your children ask for bread. Will you give them a stone? Suppose they ask for a fish. Will you give them a snake? Even though you're evil, you know how to give good gifts to your children. How much more will your Father in heaven give good gifts to those who ask him!"

One day Jesus was praying. When he finished, one of his disciples said, "Lord, teach us to pray."

Jesus said, "This is how you should pray: 'Our Father in heaven, may your name be honored. May your kingdom come soon. We pray that what you want will be done on earth as it is in heaven. Give us our food for today. Forgive us our sins, just as we forgive those who sin against us. Don't cause us to be tempted. Save us from the evil one.'"

Nicodemus
(John 3)

There was a Pharisee named Nicodemus, one of the Jewish leaders. One night he came to Jesus and said, "We know you're a teacher from God. We know God is with you. If he weren't, you wouldn't be able to do the miraculous signs you're doing."

Jesus replied, "This is the truth: No one can see God's kingdom without being born again."

"How can I be born when I'm old?" Nicodemus asked. "I can't go back inside my mother! I can't be born a second time!"

Jesus answered, "No one can come into God's kingdom without being born through water and the Holy Spirit. People give birth to people. But the Spirit gives birth to spirit. You shouldn't be surprised when I say, 'You must all be born again.'"

"How can it be possible?" Nicodemus asked.

"You're a teacher for the Israelites," said Jesus. "Don't you understand these things?

"God loved the world so much that he gave his one and only Son. Anyone who believes in him won't be lost but will have eternal life. God didn't send his Son into the world to judge it. He sent his Son to save the world through him."

Plans to Arrest Jesus

(John 7, 11)

Many people put their faith in Jesus. They said, "Surely the Messiah we are waiting for won't do more miraculous signs than this man?"

The Pharisees heard the crowd whispering this about him. It made them and the chief priests angry. They sent temple guards to arrest Jesus.

Jesus spoke in a loud voice. "If you're thirsty, come to me and drink! If you believe, rivers of living water will flow from inside you." He meant the Holy Spirit.

When the people heard him, some said, "This must be the Prophet we've been expecting." Others said, "He's the Messiah." Others asked, "Doesn't Scripture, God's book, say the Messiah will come from David's family and from Bethlehem?"

Finally the temple guards went back. The Pharisees and chief priests demanded, "Why haven't you brought him?"

"We have never heard anyone talk like this," the guards replied.

"You mean he's tricked you, too?" the Pharisees asked.

Nicodemus, the leader who had gone to Jesus earlier, spoke up. "Does our law find people guilty without hearing them first?"

They replied, "Look it up. You'll find that prophets don't come from Galilee."

Soon after, the Jewish leaders began planning to kill Jesus.

Jesus and the Children

(Matthew 18; Mark 10)

One day some parents brought their children to Jesus. They wanted him to put his hands on the children and bless them. But the disciples told the people to stop.

When Jesus saw this, he was angry. He said to his disciples, "Let the little children come to me. Don't keep them away. God's kingdom belongs to people like them. This is the truth: Anyone who doesn't have their kind of faith will never get into God's kingdom." Then he took the children in his arms. He put his hands on them and blessed them.

Another day, the disciples were trying to figure out which of them was the most important. They asked Jesus, "Who's the most important person in the kingdom of heaven?"

Jesus called a little child over to him. He had the child stand among them. Jesus said, "This is the truth: You need to change and become like little children. If you don't, you'll never get into the kingdom of heaven. Anyone who becomes as free of pride as this child is the most important in the kingdom of heaven. Anyone who welcomes a little child like this because of me welcomes me."

The Lord's Supper

(Luke 22; John 13)

It was supper time, just before the Passover holiday. Jesus and his disciples were in an upstairs room. Jesus wanted to show them how much he loved them. He wrapped a towel around his waist. He washed his disciples' feet and dried them with the towel. "Do you understand what I was doing?" Jesus asked. "I, your Lord and Teacher, washed your feet. So you also should wash each other's feet." By this, Jesus meant that we should care for each other.

Jesus continued, "I've really looked forward to eating this Passover meal with you before I suffer." Then Jesus took some bread. He gave thanks to God and broke it in pieces. He gave it to

them and said, "This is my body. It's given for you. Every time you eat it, do it to remember me."

After the supper Jesus took the cup. He said, "This cup is the new covenant, the special agreement made in my blood. I'm pouring it out for you."

Jesus was troubled deep inside, in his spirit. He said, "This is the truth: One of you is going to hand me over to those who want to kill me."

His disciples asked who it was. Jesus said, "It's the person I'm going to give this piece of bread to." He gave it to Judas Iscariot.

Judas went out into the night.

Jesus Is Arrested and Judged

(Matthew 26–27; Luke 22–23; John 18–19)

After supper, they went out to the Garden of Gethsemane. Jesus said to his disciples, "My heart is breaking with sadness!" He fell to the ground and prayed, "Father! If it's possible, let this cup of suffering be taken away from me. But I choose what you want, not what I want."

At that moment, Judas Iscariot arrived with a large crowd sent from the priests. They arrested Jesus. Jesus knew it was God's plan.

Jesus was taken to the high priest's house. Outside, a girl asked Peter, "Are you one of Jesus' close followers?" He said, "No, I'm not." This happened three times. Then Peter remembered that Jesus had said it would. He went away and cried bitterly.

Morning came and Jesus was taken to Pilate. He was the Roman leader of that area. Pilate questioned Jesus, then said to the Jews, "This man hasn't done anything to deserve death." But the Jewish leaders turned the crowd against Jesus. They shouted, "Kill him! Crucify him!" Pilate had Jesus whipped and beaten. Then he turned Jesus over to the Roman soldiers to crucify him. They put a crown of thorns and a fine robe on him and made fun of him. Then they took him away to be nailed to a cross.

Knowing that Jesus would die, Judas went away and killed himself.

Jesus Dies on the Cross

(Matthew 27; Mark 15; Luke 23; John 19)

Jesus had to carry the wooden cross to a place called Skull Hill. There the soldiers nailed him to it. Jesus said, "Father, forgive them. They don't know what they're doing."

They crucified two robbers with him. One of them made fun of Jesus. He said, "Aren't you God's Chosen One, the Messiah? Save yourself! Save us!"

But the other said, "Don't you have any respect for God? This man hasn't done anything wrong." Then he said, "Jesus, remember me when you come into your kingdom."

Jesus answered, "This is the truth: Today you'll be with me in paradise."

At midday, darkness covered the whole land. It lasted three hours. Jesus cried out in a loud voice, "My God, my God, why have you left me?" Then he took his last breath.

A Roman army commander standing nearby said, "This man was surely the Son of God!"

That evening Joseph, a follower of Jesus, went bravely to Pilate and asked for Jesus' body. Nicodemus, the man who had visited Jesus at night, went with him. They wrapped Jesus' body in some fine cloth. Then they put it in a new tomb cut in the rock nearby.

Jesus Rises from the Dead

(Matthew 28; Mark 16; Luke 24; John 20)

Very early on Sunday morning, some women went to the tomb.

There was a powerful earthquake. An angel of the Lord came down from heaven, shining like lightning. He went to the tomb, rolled back the stone, and sat on it. He said to them, "Don't be afraid. I know you're looking for Jesus, who died on the cross. He's not here! He has risen to life again! Go! Tell his disciples, 'He's risen from the dead.'"

The women told the eleven disciples, but they didn't believe them. That same day Jesus' followers were talking about this when

Jesus himself suddenly stood among them. He said, "May peace be with you!"

They were very frightened. They thought they were seeing a ghost!

Jesus said, "Why do you doubt who I am? Touch me and see. A ghost doesn't have a body or bones. But I do." They were amazed and filled with joy. Jesus said, "Everything written about me in Moses' Law, the Prophets' writings, and the Psalms had to come true."

Then they understood that he was the one God had promised. He'd died so people could have peace with God and enjoy his love again.

Jesus Returns to Heaven

(Matthew 28; Luke 24; Acts 1)

Forty days passed after God raised Jesus from the dead. In this time, Jesus was often seen by the disciples.

He gave them an order. He said, "I've been given the right to rule over all heaven and earth. So go and make disciples of all the nations. Baptize them in the name of the Father, the Son, and the Holy Spirit. Teach them to obey all the commands I've given you.

"But don't leave Jerusalem until the Holy Spirit comes and fills you with power from heaven," Jesus said. "And be sure of this: I'm always with you, right to the end of time."

On the fortieth day, Jesus led his disciples out of the city. He lifted up his hands and blessed them. While he was blessing them, he was taken up to heaven. They watched until a cloud hid him.

Suddenly, two men dressed in white stood among them. "Why are you standing here staring at the sky?" they asked. "Jesus has been taken away from you into heaven. And someday he'll come back in the same way!"

The disciples worshiped the Lord, and, full of joy, they returned to Jerusalem.

Pentecost

(Acts 2)

Seven weeks later was the Jewish holiday of
Pentecost. Those who believed in Jesus were praying
together in Jerusalem. Suddenly a sound like a
strong wind filled the house. Something like tongues
of fire came upon each of them. They were filled
with the Holy Spirit. They began to speak in
languages they hadn't known before. The Holy Spirit
gave them the words.

People from many different countries lived in
Jerusalem at that time. Now they gathered because of
the sound. They were amazed to hear their own
languages being spoken and wondered how it could
be possible. Others thought the believers were drunk.

Peter explained, "What you see today was
foretold centuries ago by the prophet Joel. He wrote,
'In the last days,' God said, 'I'll pour out my Spirit on
all people. Your sons and daughters will prophesy. I'll
show wonders in the heavens and miraculous signs
on the earth. And everyone who calls on the name of
the Lord will be saved.'

"God did wonderful miracles through Jesus,"
Peter continued. "You nailed him to the cross. But
God has made him both Lord and Messiah."

The people were deeply moved, and they felt guilty.
"Brothers," they cried out, "what should we do?"

Peter replied, "Turn away from your sins, return
to God, and be baptized in the name of Jesus Christ.
Then you'll be forgiven. You'll receive the gift of the
Holy Spirit. This promise is for you and your
children, and all their children to come."

About 3,000 people joined the believers that day.

The Church Is Born

(Acts 2, 4)

The disciples who'd been sent out first were now called apostles. They taught the new believers all about Jesus so they would also become disciples, or true followers. This was just what Jesus had told them to do.

The believers studied what the apostles taught. They shared life together. Every day they met in the temple courtyard. And they prayed and praised God. They broke bread in their homes to remember Jesus, and they ate together. Their hearts were glad and

honest and true. All the believers were of one heart and mind. They didn't claim that anything they had was their own. They shared everything. No one was poor because those who owned land or houses sold them. They brought the money to the apostles. It was then given to anyone who needed it.

The apostles did many wonders and miraculous signs. Boldly, they gave witness that the Lord Jesus had risen from the dead.

God's great favor was upon them all. Everyone liked them. And each day the Lord added to their group more people who were being saved.

Peter and Cornelius

(Acts 10–11)

One day, Peter had a vision. He saw a large sheet being let down to earth with all kinds of animals, reptiles (like snakes and lizards), and birds in it. A voice told him, "Get up, Peter. Kill and eat them."

"No, Lord!" Peter replied. "I've never eaten anything that Moses' Law says isn't clean."

The voice said, "God has made them pure. Don't call them unclean."

Then the Holy Spirit spoke to him. "Three men are downstairs looking for you," he said. "I've sent them."

The men told Peter, "We've come from Cornelius, the Roman army commander. He's a good man who respects God. An angel told him to invite you to his home. He wants to hear what you have to say." So Peter went with the men.

After a day's journey, they arrived. While Peter was talking about Jesus, the Holy Spirit came on all who heard. They spoke in tongues—languages they hadn't known before—and praised God.

The Jewish believers had thought Jesus, their Messiah, had died only for Jews. Now they were excited. They saw everyone could turn from their sins and get a new life with God.

Saul Believes

(Acts 6–9)

Stephen was a man who did amazing miracles. But some Jews who weren't believers started causing trouble. After having him questioned, they threw stones at him until he was dead. A young man named Saul looked on and agreed with what they were doing.

After this, Saul had the high priest write some letters to the Jewish leaders in Damascus, a city outside Israel. The letters allowed him to take believers as prisoners to Jerusalem. As Saul came near Damascus, suddenly a light from heaven flashed around him! He fell to the ground. He heard a voice say, "Saul! Why are you fighting me?"

"Who are you, Lord?" Saul asked.

"I'm Jesus," he replied. "Go into the city." Saul got up. But he was blind.

Three days later, the Lord spoke to a believer named Ananias, "Ananias! Go to the house of Judas, the one who lives on Straight Street. Ask for Saul. He's praying. In a vision he's seen a man called Ananias coming and laying his hands on him so he'll see again." Ananias did as he was told. Immediately, Saul could see again. He got up and was baptized.

Saul became one of Jesus' best-known followers.

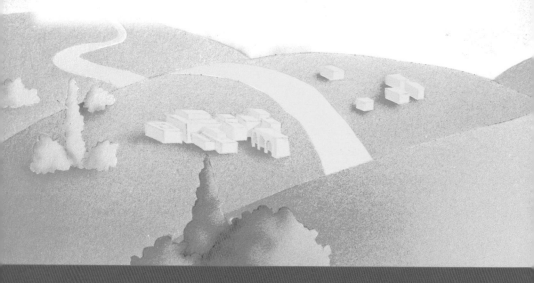

The Gentiles Hear the Good News

(Acts 11, 13–14)

Saul traveled with a believer called Barnabas to Antioch, a faraway city. While the church there was worshiping the Lord and fasting (going without food), the Holy Spirit spoke. "Set apart for me Barnabas and Saul for the special work I have for them," he said. So the leaders of the church laid their hands on them and sent them on their way.

Barnabas and Saul (also called Paul) traveled further, going first to Jewish meeting places.

Paul said, "What God promised to Abraham, Isaac, Jacob, and David, he has now done. Your sins can be forgiven. Through Jesus everyone who believes is made right with God." Many Jews and non-Jews followed them. But some Jews became jealous.

Paul and Barnabas told them, "We had to speak God's message to you first. But you don't believe it. So we'll tell the non-Jews, the Gentiles, as the Lord commanded us."

When the Gentiles heard this they were very glad.

The Lord's message spread. Paul and Barnabas spoke boldly. The Lord gave them the ability to do miracles and wonders. In this way the Lord showed that they were telling the truth.

Paul went on three journeys to tell God's message and started churches in many cities. Later he wrote letters to the churches, teaching them more about how to live as Christians.

The Meeting in Jerusalem

(Acts 15)

The believers had found out that everyone could become a Christian. But then some Jews came to the city of Antioch teaching that Gentile, non-Jewish, believers had to live like Jews to be saved.

Paul and Barnabas argued strongly with them. So the church sent them to Jerusalem to see the apostles and elders. They had a meeting to discuss this question.

Peter reminded everyone about Cornelius. He said, "God knows people's hearts. By giving the Holy Spirit to Gentiles, he showed he welcomes them, too. He made their hearts pure through their faith. Why are you testing God by making life hard for his followers? No! We believe we Jews are saved as a free gift from our Lord Jesus. Non-Jews are saved the same way."

James spoke up. "Brothers, we shouldn't trouble Gentiles who are turning to God. We shouldn't make them keep the Jewish Law."

So they sent Paul, Barnabas, and others back to Antioch with a letter explaining this. The people in Antioch were glad for its encouraging message.

Letter to the Galatians

(Galatians 3, 5)

On their first journey, Paul and Barnabas started several churches in an area called Galatia, now in Turkey. Later, he heard disturbing news. The people were trying to keep the religious laws again!

"Have you gone crazy?" he wrote them. "Does God give you the Holy Spirit and work miracles among you because you obey Moses' Law? Of course not! It's because you believe in Jesus—that he loved you and gave himself for you. So stop thinking that you will be saved by keeping the Law! That Law was like a baby-sitter to watch over us and tell us what to do until Jesus came. But now, when you believe in Jesus, only one thing counts: your faith, which shows itself in love for God and other people. The old, sinful 'you' likes to be bad, but the Holy Spirit makes you want just the opposite. There's a fight inside you!

"Listen now to the new commandment, all of you: 'Love your neighbor like you love yourself.' Let the Holy Spirit be your teacher, not religious laws. Then your lives will show his fruit, because he produces it.

"What's his fruit? It's love, joy, and peace. It's being patient, kind, good, faithful, and gentle, and it's having control of your wants and feelings."

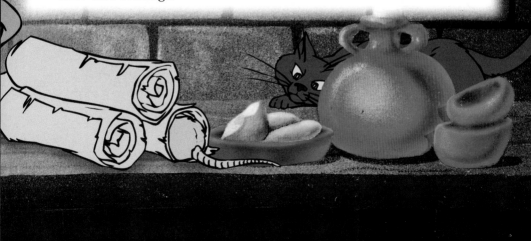

159

Letter to the Romans

(Romans 1, 8)

Paul hadn't been to Rome, Italy, the capital of the Roman Empire. During his third journey, he wrote this letter to believers there:

"I'm not ashamed of the good news," he wrote. "It's God's power at work, saving everyone who believes—Jews first and also non-Jews. This good news tells us how God makes us right with him. From start to finish, this happens by our faith in him.

"We know that God makes everything work together for the good of those who love him. Then since God is on our side, who can be against us? God didn't even keep back his own Son. He gave him for us all. Then won't he also freely give us everything else?

"Who can separate us from Jesus' love? Does it mean he no longer loves us if we have trouble or hard times? No! In all these things we win an amazing victory! We owe it all to Jesus, who loved us. I'm absolutely, totally sure that nothing at all can ever take us away from God's love. Death can't, and life can't. The angels can't, and the wicked spirits can't. Nothing will ever be able to separate us from God's love, which he showed in Christ Jesus, our Lord."

Letter to the Corinthians—One Body

(1 Corinthians 3, 12)

Corinth is a city in Greece. Paul started the church in Corinth on his second journey. Later the Corinthians got jealous of each other and started to disagree about who was the best church leader. They wrote to Paul for help. He replied that they must stop acting like babies. He explained that God wants the church to work like a body.

"Your human body has many parts, but they make up only one body. Christ's body here on earth is the same. Christ's body is now

made up of believers. We're all different, but we all belong together. Suppose your ear says, 'I'm not a body part because I'm not an eye.' It's still part of the body! If your whole body were one big eye, how would you hear? What a strange thing your body would be if it only had one part!

"And the head can't say to the feet, 'I don't need you!' In fact, the body parts that seem weaker are the ones you can't do without.

"So God has joined all the parts. Together, you believers are Christ's body. Each one of you is a part of it. Ask God to make you even more useful to the others."

Letter to the Corinthians—Love

(1 Corinthians 13; 2 Corinthians 5)

The Christians in Corinth needed to learn to love one another. So Paul wrote to them about real love.

"Suppose I speak in the languages of humans and angels. If I don't love others, I'm like a loud banging or a noisy crashing. Suppose God gives me the ability to tell others what he's saying, I understand his secret things, and I have faith to move mountains. If I don't have love, I'm nothing at all. Suppose I give away everything I have to poor people and give my body to be burned. If I don't do it because I love others, I'm of no use at all.

"Love is patient and kind. Love isn't jealous or boastful or proud or rude. With real love, I don't demand my own way. I don't get angry easily. I don't bother about the wrong things people have done to me.

"Love isn't glad about wickedness. It's full of joy whenever the truth wins out. Love always protects others, always believes, always hopes. It never gives up.

"Love will last forever."

Only Christians with God's Holy Spirit can love this way. So Paul wrote, "Anyone who becomes a Christian is a new person inside. The old life has gone! A new life has begun!"

Letters from Prison

(Ephesians 6; Philippians 4)

Paul was put in prison for preaching the gospel, the good news about Jesus. But nothing could stop him! From prison, he wrote letters to other churches.

"Let the Lord and his mighty power make you strong. Put on all God's armor. Then you'll be able to stand firm against the devil's evil plans. Our fight isn't against people. It's against the powerful wicked spirits in the world you can't see.

"Hold on to the truth. That's your belt. To guard your heart, put on the breastplate of being right with God. Wear on your feet shoes that will prepare you to tell the good news of peace. Trust in God. That's your shield of faith against the devil's attacks. It will put out all his fiery arrows. Remember that God saved you and welcomed you. That's your helmet. And strike back at the devil with God's Word. That's the sword of the Spirit.

"At all times, pray by the Holy Spirit's power."

Paul even wrote from prison about freedom and joy: "Always be joyful because you're the Lord's! I'll say it again. Be joyful!

"Don't worry about anything. Instead, pray about everything. Tell God what you need, and give him thanks. Then God's peace will guard your hearts and minds."

Letters to Paul's Helpers

(1 Timothy 6; 2 Timothy 1–3; Titus 2)

Paul liked to have helpers as he spread the gospel about Jesus. Timothy and Titus were two of these. Paul loved them. He called Timothy his son. He carefully trained them to work in the churches in different places. When he was old, Paul wrote them letters:

"Live life for God and be happy that way. Run from evil things, and follow what's right and good. Have faith, love, and gentleness. Fight the good fight for what you believe. Hold tightly to the eternal life that God has given you, while you wait for Jesus to return.

"God didn't give us a spirit that's weak and fearful. He gave us a spirit of power, love, and self-control. So don't be ashamed to tell others about our Lord.

"You've known God's Scriptures since you were little. They have given you wisdom to be saved by trusting in Jesus. God has breathed life into all Scripture. It's useful to teach us what's true and make us realize what's wrong in our lives. By using Scripture, we can be ready for everything God wants us to do."

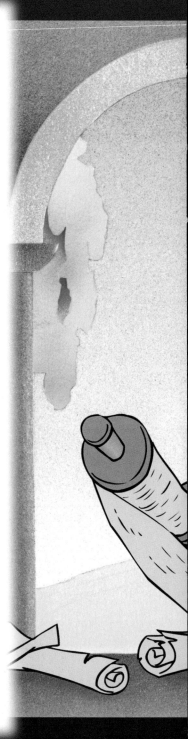

Letter from James

(James 1–5)

Jesus' brother James was a leader of the Jerusalem church. James wrote a letter for believers living in different places.

"Wisdom means knowing what God wants you to do. If you need wisdom, ask God for it. He'll gladly give it to you.

"Everyone should be quick to listen, slow to speak, and slow to get angry. But don't just listen to God's message. Do what it says! Otherwise, you're only tricking yourself. What good is it if people say they believe but don't act like it?

"Ships are big. But they're steered by a small rudder. In the same way, the tongue is small. But no one can control it. Out of the same mouth comes both praise and unkind words. That's not right!

"Obey God. Stand against the devil. He'll run away from you! Come near to God, and he'll come near to you.

"If you're sick, ask the leaders of the church to pray for you and pour a little oil on you. Their prayer offered in faith will make you well. If you've done wrong, you'll be forgiven.

"Pray for each other. Because God has made you right with him, your prayers are powerful and bring wonderful results."

Letter from Peter

(1 Peter 1–2, 4–5; 2 Peter 3)

Do you remember how Peter said three times he wasn't Jesus' follower? Jesus forgave him. Peter became one of the main leaders in the church. He was the first one to tell the gospel to non-Jews. He wrote letters to Christians in a large area known today as Turkey. Later, Peter was killed because he was a faithful follower of Jesus. Peter wrote:

"Be very glad! There's wonderful joy ahead, even though it's necessary for you to go through many troubles for a while. Your troubles are only to prove your faith is real. It's worth more to God than gold.

"The blood of Christ set you free. So get rid of every kind of evil behavior. Stop telling lies. Don't pretend to be something you're not. Stop wanting what others have. Above all, love one another deeply.

"Scripture says, 'God is against those who are proud. But he shows his goodness to those who are not.' Turn all your worries over to him. He cares about you.

"Live for God as you look forward to the day when Jesus will come back. He's promised us a new heaven and a new earth."

Letter from John

(1 John 1–5)

John the fisherman became a leader of the first church. He lived the longest of all the apostles. He was called "the disciple Jesus loved." He wrote a lot about love, too:

"Dear children, let's not just say we love each other, let's show it by our actions. Let's love one another, because love comes from God. Everyone who loves has been born of God and knows God. Anyone who doesn't love doesn't know God, because God is love. What is love? It's not that we loved God. It's that he loved us and sent his Son to give his life to pay for our sins.

"No one has ever seen God. But if we love one another, God lives in us, and his love can be seen through us.

"There's no fear in love. Instead, perfect love drives fear away."

John also wrote about other things, such as God's forgiveness and willingness to answer prayer:

"God is faithful and fair. If we admit that we've sinned, he'll forgive us. He'll make us clean again.

"I write this to you who believe in the Son of God, so you may know you have everlasting life. If we ask God for anything we know he wants for us, he hears us. And if we know he hears us, then what we asked for is already ours."

God Judges All People

(Revelation 1, 19–21)

John was sent to a prison camp on an island far away because he preached the gospel. One day he was praying. Suddenly an angel from God came. He showed him many things. John saw what will happen in the future:

"I saw heaven standing open. There in front of me was a white horse. Its rider was named Faithful and True. His eyes were like flames of fire, and on his head were many crowns. The armies of heaven followed him. He struck down the nations that were against God.

"An angel came down. He grabbed that old snake called the devil, or Satan, and threw him into a bottomless pit. Then Jesus reigned on the earth for 1,000 years. After this, the devil was thrown into the lake of fire. He'll be in awful pain forever and ever.

"I saw a great white throne and the one who was sitting on it. I saw all who had died. They were standing in front of the throne. The things they had done were written in books. From these, God judged them. Anyone whose name wasn't in the Book of Life was thrown into the lake of fire."

A New Heaven and a New Earth

(Revelation 21–22)

"Then I saw a new heaven and a new earth," John wrote. "And I saw the holy city, the new Jerusalem. It came down from God out of heaven like a beautiful bride. The city doesn't need the sun or moon. God's glory is its light. And Jesus, the Lamb of God, is its lamp. Only those whose names are written in the Lamb's Book of Life will go in."

A loud voice said, "Look! God's home is now among his people. He'll live with them. He'll wipe away every tear from their eyes. There'll be no more death or sadness or crying or pain."

The one on the throne said, "Look, I'm making everything new! It is finished. I am the Beginning and the End. Anyone who's thirsty may drink. It costs nothing to drink from the spring of the water of life. Those who win the good fight will receive all this. I'll be their God, and they'll be my children."

Then Jesus said to John, "See, I'm coming soon! I'll reward each of you for what you've done."

The Holy Spirit says, "Come!"

Let those who hear say, "Come!"

Amen. Come, Lord Jesus!

The Adventure Begins

You've just finished reading some special stories from God's book, the Bible. You learned how God created men and women, how they made the choice in the Garden of Eden to sin by not following him, and what the results were. But God sent Jesus into the world to die for the sins of all people, and the New Testament church preached that good news to the world. The last two stories were about things that haven't happened yet: how Jesus will return to earth soon and how those who believe and welcome him will be with him forever.

This children's Bible describes the adventures of amazing men and women of God—kings, queens, shepherds, soldiers, fishermen, and carpenters—who lived in different countries in different cultures. Some of these people lived hundreds or even thousands of years apart. But the Bible isn't just a collection of wonderful stories. No! All these are part of one big story—the story of God's plan for everyone who has ever lived.

God loves every single person on earth and he wants all of us to be with him forever. In "The Most Important Story Ever Told" you'll find out about the wonderful plan God has for you, and how you can make sure you'll be with him forever.

The MOST IMPORTANT Story EVER TOLD

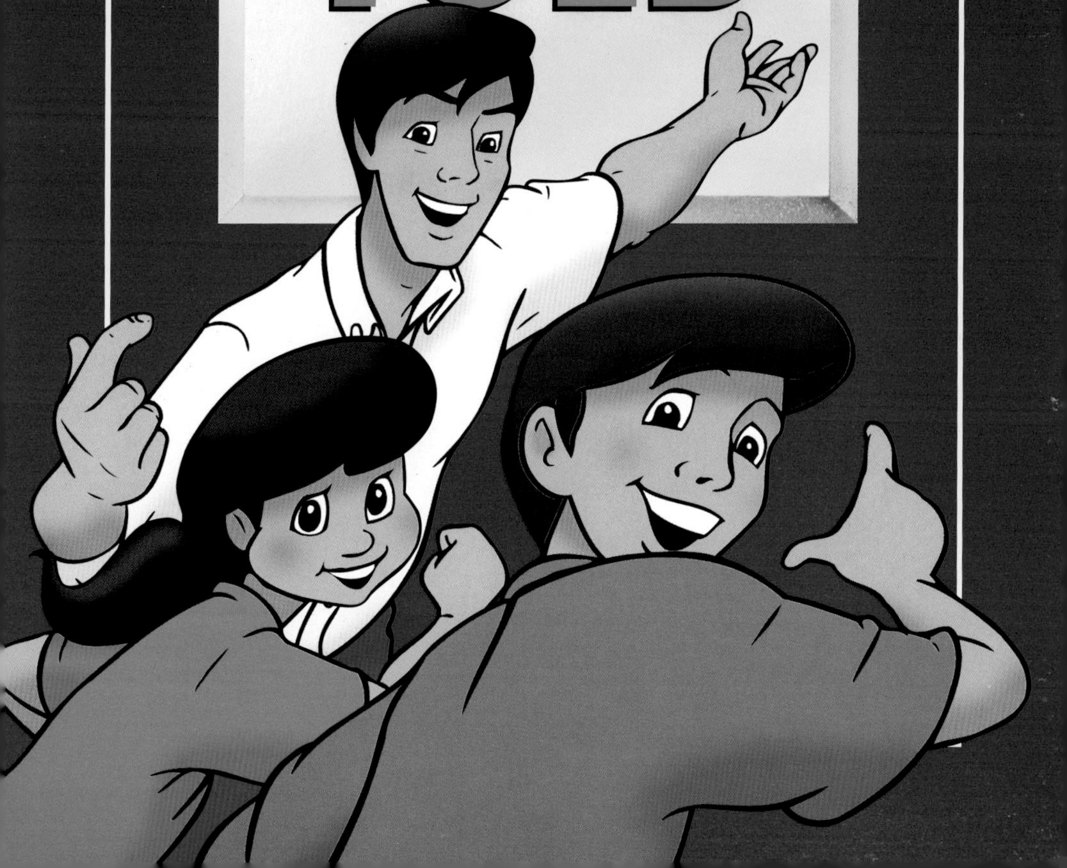

Creation—
Adam and Eve

Bible Reference: Genesis 1, 2

God said, "Let us make people in our image, to be like ourselves." And the LORD God formed a man's body from the dust of the ground and breathed into it the breath of life. And the man became a living person.

"Dust?"

"Right, Matt. God can do anything!"

Then God said, "It is not good for the man to be alone. I will make a partner who will help him." So the LORD God caused Adam to fall into a deep sleep. He took one of Adam's ribs and made a woman from the rib.

God brought the woman, Eve, to Adam as his wife.

At the center of the garden God placed the tree of life and the tree of the knowledge of good and evil. But the LORD God gave the man this warning: "You may freely eat any fruit in the garden except fruit from the tree of the knowledge of good and evil. If you eat of its fruit, you will surely die."

Adam and Eve lived in the garden and they were very happy. They were close to God and enjoyed being with him. But one day . . .

Adam and Eve Sin

Bible Reference: Genesis 3

Satan, God's enemy, disguised himself as a serpent. He didn't want Adam and Eve to be with God and obey him.

He asked Eve, "Did God really say you must not eat any of the fruit in the garden?"

She told him, "It's only the fruit from the tree at the center of the garden that we are not allowed to eat. God says we must not eat it or even touch it, or we will die."

"You won't die!" the serpent hissed. "You will become just like God."

The woman was convinced. The fruit looked so fresh and delicious, and it would make her so wise! So she . . .

"NO! Don't eat it, Eve!"

"Good advice, Matt. But she did, and so did Adam."

Suddenly, they were afraid. They hid from God when he came to walk in the garden. They had sinned by choosing to disobey God. So he sent them away—out of the Garden of Eden.

God loved Adam and Eve. He wanted them to have a choice, to choose for themselves to love and obey him. But they chose to disobey God. They didn't know how awful separation from God would be.

And, because they chose to sin, everyone who came after them was born sinful and separated from God, too.

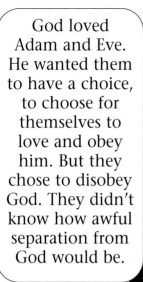

You mean we can't be with God because of them? That's not fair!

Not only because of them, Matt. We all sin when we do wrong things. But don't worry. God had a wonderful plan to bring us back to him. He just needed one perfect person.

When everything was ready God put his plan into action. It began with a baby!

Jesus Is Born

Bible Reference: Matthew 1, Luke 2

God gave Mary his own Son as a baby. He chose Joseph to help Mary look after him. Because the baby was God's Son, he was born without sin.

An angel of the Lord appeared to Joseph in a dream. The angel said, "Mary will have a son, and you are to name him Jesus, for he will save his people from their sins." (Jesus means "the Lord saves.")

Just before the baby was born, Joseph and Mary

had to go to Bethlehem.

While they were there, Mary gave birth to her first child, a son.

God sent angels to tell people about his Son's birth. They came to see this amazing event: God's Son born as a baby!

"Jesus grew up like you kids."

"Did he go to school, Dad? And play?"

"Yes, Matt. He also obeyed his parents, and was obedient to his real Father, God. And he never sinned!"

Jesus the Teacher

Bible Reference: Luke 2, Matthew 22, John 3

When he was 12 years old, Jesus was in Jerusalem with the teachers.

He was in the temple discussing deep questions with them. And all who heard him were amazed at his understanding and his answers.

Jesus grew both in height and in wisdom, and he was loved by God and by all who knew him.

When he was 30, Jesus started to preach and teach. He taught that God cares how people think and act. And he said,"**You must love the Lord your God with all your heart, all your soul, and all your mind.' This is the first and greatest commandment. A second is equally important: 'Love your neighbor as yourself.'**"

Jesus told about God's wonderful plan to bring us back to him.

He said, **"God so loved the world that he gave his only Son, so that everyone who believes in him will not perish but have eternal life."**

"I believe in Jesus, Dad!"
"That's great, Erica!"

192

Jesus the Healer

Bible Reference: Matthew 4, 9

Jesus also helped people see what God is like. He showed them God loves them. One way he did this was by healing every kind of sickness and disease.

The sick were soon coming to be healed. And whatever their illness and pain, or if they were possessed by demons, or were epileptics, or were paralyzed— Jesus healed them all.

One time, a ruler got down on his knees in front of Jesus.

"My daughter has just died," he said, **"but you can bring her back to life again if you just come and lay your hand upon her."**

Jesus went and took the girl by the hand, and she stood up!

"Wow! Jesus really healed people, Dad?"

"That's right, Matt. And he still heals today. Nothing is too hard for him!"

Jesus the Miracle Worker

Bible Reference: Matthew 14, John 6

"Jesus did other wonderful and amazing things. He calmed storms and walked on water!"

"That must have been exciting!"

"It was, Matt. Another time, more than 5,000 people followed Jesus to a distant place. His friends and followers, the disciples, wanted to send the hungry people away to buy food for themselves, because it was late."

Jesus replied, "That isn't necessary—you feed them."

Andrew spoke up. "There's a youngster here with five barley loaves and two fish! But what good is that with this huge crowd?"

Jesus took the loaves, gave thanks to God, and passed them out to the people. Afterward he did the same with the fish. And they all ate until they were full!

"Now gather the leftovers," Jesus told his disciples, "so that nothing is wasted."

There were only five barley loaves to start with, but twelve baskets were filled with the pieces of bread the people did not eat!

"There were more leftovers than the food they started with?"

"Right, Erica. Jesus was teaching them God can meet all their needs. He'll do the same for us when we ask him."

Jesus and the Children

Bible Reference: Matthew 19, Mark 10

"Jesus showed people that God loves children. He healed them, let them help him (like the boy with the food), and even raised them from the dead!"

Some children were brought to Jesus so he could lay his hands on them and pray for them. The disciples told the people not to bother him.

When Jesus saw what was happening, he said, "Let the children come to me. Don't stop them! Anyone who

doesn't have their kind of faith will never get into the
kingdom of God." Then he took the children into his arms
and placed his hands on their heads and blessed them.

"I want to be blessed by Jesus, too!"

"You can be, Matt. Jesus is the same today and he
loves children just as much."

"Not everyone liked him, though. What he did and
taught made the religious leaders angry. They were
jealous that the people liked him too much. So they
planned to get rid of him."

Jesus' Arrest and Trial

Bible Reference: Luke 22, John 19

"One night, when Jesus was talking to his friends, the religious leaders sent a crowd with clubs and swords."

The disciples exclaimed, "Lord, should we fight? We brought the swords!" And one of them slashed at a servant and cut off his right ear.

But Jesus said, "Don't resist any more." And he touched the place where the man's ear had been and healed him.

"Jesus healed one of his enemies?"

"Yes, Erica. He loves everyone."

They grabbed Jesus and arrested him. They took him to the ruler of the area, Pilate, and put him on trial. The soldiers beat Jesus, put thorns on his head, and made fun of him. Then Pilate spoke to the people.

"I am going to bring him out to you now, but understand clearly that I find him not guilty."

"Away with him," they yelled. "Crucify him!"

Then Pilate gave Jesus to them to be crucified.

"But he didn't do anything wrong! That's not fair!"

"Right, Matt. But remember, God had a plan."

Jesus Dies on the Cross

Bible Reference: Luke 23

"They nailed Jesus to the cross."

Jesus said, "Father, forgive these people, because they don't know what they are doing."

Two others, both criminals, were executed with him. One of the criminals hanging beside him scoffed, "So you're the Messiah, are you?" (Messiah is another name for the Son of God.) "Prove it by saving yourself—and us, too, while you're at it!"

But the other criminal protested, "Don't you fear God even when you are dying? We deserve to die for our evil deeds, but this man hasn't done anything wrong." Then he said, "Jesus, remember me when you come into your kingdom."

Jesus replied, "I assure you, today you will be with me in paradise."

"He got to be with Jesus after he died?"

"Right, Erica!

"Later, Jesus cried out to his Father, God, and died."

"Hey, is Jesus the person in God's plan?"

"Right, Matt. God sent his own perfect Son, Jesus. And he died to take the punishment for our sins."

Jesus Is Alive

Bible Reference: Matthew 28, Luke 24

Jesus' body was put in a tomb by his friends.
Early on the first day of the week two women went
to the tomb.

Suddenly there was a great earthquake, because an
angel of the Lord came down from heaven and rolled
aside the stone from the tomb.

"Don't be afraid," he said. "I know you are looking
for Jesus, who was crucified. He isn't here! He has been
raised from the dead, just as he said would happen.

Now go quickly and tell his disciples."

"That's the best part!"

"Right, Matt! After he'd paid for our sins, God raised him from the dead. That was God's plan all along."

Later, as the disciples were talking about it, **Jesus** himself was suddenly standing there among them. He said, "Peace be with you." But the whole group was terribly frightened, thinking they were seeing a ghost!

"Why are you frightened?" he asked. "Look at my hands. Look at my feet. You can see that it's really me. Touch me and make sure that I am not a ghost!"

Where Is Jesus Today?

Bible Reference: John 16, Acts 1

"Jesus was with his disciples for many weeks."

"They must have been happy!"

"Yes, but where's Jesus now?"

"Good question, Erica."

Jesus said, **"It is actually best for you that I go away, because if I don't, the Holy Spirit won't come. If I do go away, he will come, because I will send him to you."**

When Jesus had finished speaking with the disciples, they watched him rise into the sky and disappear into a cloud. Two angels told them, **"Jesus has been taken away from you into heaven. And someday, just as you saw him go, he will return!"**

One day Jesus will come back for all God's children. That's everyone who believes Jesus died for them and has been forgiven. We will be with him forever. Nothing will ever separate us from God's love again!

I want to be God's child, so I can be with him.

That's great, Matt! This is the most important decision you'll ever make! The Bible tells us our sin separates us from God. And it says, "If you confess with your mouth that Jesus is Lord and believe in your heart that God raised him from the dead, you will be saved. For it is by believing in your heart that you are made right with God, and it is by confessing with your mouth that you are saved."
Romans 10:9–10

I can say that! I really do believe in Jesus!

Then let's tell God. He's always listening, Matt. He hears our prayers and answers us. Say this prayer with me.

Dear God, I know I'm a sinner. I made wrong choices and did bad things. I'm sorry. Please forgive me. I know your Son, Jesus, died for my sins, and I believe you raised him from the dead. I want Jesus to be my Lord. Thank you for loving me and making me your child. Now, please fill me with your Holy Spirit, so I'll have all the strength I need to obey you. Amen.

If you prayed with Matt, you've made the most important decision and started the greatest adventure of all. Write your name and the date here so you'll always remember:

"I, _____, became God's

child today." Date: _____

To continue on in your greatest adventure:

- Pray. Talk to God from your heart about anything, anytime, anywhere.

- Get a Bible and begin reading it. Try starting with the book of Mark, then Acts and James. Then just keep reading.

- Tell your friends what has happened to you. They can become God's children too.

- Find a local church where they love Jesus and where the Bible is taught. You'll meet more of God's children and learn about God.